Science & Religion at the Crossroads

Frank Parkinson

ia

IMPRINT ACADEMIC

Published in the UK by
Imprint Academic, PO Box 200, Exeter EX5 5YX, UK

Published in the USA by
Imprint Academic, Philosophy Documentation Center
PO Box 7147, Charlottesville, VA 22906-7147, USA

ISBN 9781845401511

A CIP catalogue record for this book is available from
the British Library and US Library of Congress.

Contents

Part 2:

LOOKING FORWARD: NEOSCIENCE

Part 3:

LOOKING FORWARD: NEOTHEOLOGY

Part 4:

STRIKING OUT

Acknowledgements

Two of the pieces in this collection appeared originally in journals and are reprinted in revised or abridged form with permission. Thanks are due to the editors as follows:

"Classical Christianity as an Obstacle to Truth", Faith and Freedom: A Journal of Progressive Religion, Vol 55, Part 1, 2002.

"The Dawkins Phenomenon," *Scientific and Medical Network Review*, Winter 2007.

The following essays originated as talks given to different groups, and have benefited from questions raised at the time and subsequent discussions on their themes.

"Beyond Einstein" is the expanded transcript of a paper delivered to the Science and Religion Forum Conference on *Einstein, God and Time* at the Clarendon Laboratory, Oxford, 13/9/2005.

"Neurotheology and Free Will" originated in a short talk, "Spirituality Today", given at the June 2nd, 2007 meeting of the Yorkshire branch of the Scientific and Medical Network.

"Cosmotheology" is an expanded version of a talk with the same title given to CANA (Christians Awakening to a New Awareness) at Birmingham University, Dec. 8, 2006.

"Towards a Unified Understanding" is a revised and expanded version of an invited address given at the Unitarian Church, Blackpool, June 20, 2004.

INTRODUCTION

This book is about evolution and the future of the human family, but more particularly about the future of science and religion. Both, it argues, are in a critical and unstable state – at a crossroads – because both are now facing paradigmatic change. The collection of papers which make up the book deal with different aspects of the change required, and while its prime intention is to raise awareness, in some places it does suggest useful, even necessary, answers to the problems that are identified. Some of the papers are revised versions of previous talks and articles, some have been written specially for this volume, to fill in gaps and tie complex themes into a unity. Inevitably, there was some repetition in the originals, and this has been largely edited out, but occasionally left in deliberately where it seemed to give useful emphasis.

The title of the book was chosen to indicate that both science and religion now find themselves a point of decision, where difficult choices must be made. Though both still retain social authority, they are losing prestige and moral influence, albeit for different reasons, and since there is no way back, the only way is forward, by facing up to new discoveries for which explanation cannot be found within the current framework of understanding. Upon inspection it will be found that many of the problems now arising are common to both science and religion, and, as always, identifying them takes us more than half way to their solutions. What we are learning about cosmic and biological evolution, about brain function and the historical origin of religion must stir curiosity in all but the most reactionary scientist and religionist. Somewhere in this vast, and growing, area of knowledge a new definition of the traditional "God" must be found and a post-Cartesian definition of science, able to encompass a reality beyond its traditional three dimensions.

The book is structured in four parts. The first, "At the Crossroads," functions more or less as an overview, showing why and how science and religion have arrived at the present juncture.

The second part, "Looking Forward: Neoscience," contains two essays dealing with physical science and indicating why Hubble's discovery of the galactic redshift has made Einsteinian orthodoxy out of date and counter-productive.

The third part, "Looking Forward: Neotheology," sketches a new theological framework, based on recent discoveries from several scientific fields, within which the nature of spirituality can be explored. The word "sketch" should perhaps be emphasized, for this collection is only the introduction to the grandest of themes. It should be approached as a series of dots which the reader can join up over time, to get some idea of a future of great optimism for both science and religion.

The last part, "Striking Out," puts up two signposts, as it were, to indicate the direction of religious progress, namely the need to recognize that we are a single species, a global family, and to accept that the creation story now being opened up by science must be the core myth of authentic future religion.

Given so many gaps and controversial proposals, there is almost unlimited scope for misunderstanding, and to minimize this as far as possible, it would be advisable to make explicit the major assumptions that underlie its different parts and give them unity. The first and most fundamental is that human evolution is a process of advance from lower to higher consciousness, an assertion which might seem obvious to some, but will be contested by those who insist that value judgements must be kept out of science. In a purely mechanical science, this would be a good principle to follow, but not when one wishes to understand human evolution.

The reasons for this constitutes a second assumption, namely that the human species is unique in being able to transform itself, and raising awareness of this fact is the immediate challenge now facing us. To quote from Edward O. Wilson,

> *Homo sapiens*, the first truly free species, is about to decommission natural selection, the force that made us .... Soon we must look deep within ourselves and decide what we wish to become.[1]

From this it follows that until we have some idea of the higher kind of consciousness towards which evolution is tending, we shall be unable to move forward. We shall either mill around or go off in a direction that will ultimately prove to be, at best, a blind alley or, at worst, damaging to our species and the planet.

A third assumption is that both science and religion evolve, which needs to be stressed, since it is by no means a common understanding. Most practising scientists have little knowledge of when, how or why the discipline that was first called natural philosophy came into being, and when it changed its name to science. They would probably be surprised to learn that the word "scientist" was only invented in 1833 and its use was, in fact, strongly resisted for a good many years. Few scientists today would consider themselves to be philosophers, as once they did, and this lack of thinking at philosophical depth is leading to science being broken into non-connecting fragments, and to scientism, a parody of genuine science, more akin to religious fundamentalism than to the openmindedness and sense of a common quest that once was characteristic of science.

In parallel with the intellectual shallowness of much science, even at universities, most religionists have no sense of either the historical antecedents of their belief system or its philosophical underpinning. In general a faith is taken to be fixed in doctrine and practice and those who subscribe to it usually consider their particular version of religion as the best. The Jews regard themselves as the chosen people, God's "unique treasure," as the Old Testament puts it, Moslems are unquestionably sure that Mohamed was the "last and greatest of the prophets," outranking Jesus, whom Christians worship as the "only begotten son of God," and so on. Buddhists, however humble, believe they are more advanced than theists, because they have escaped from the delusion that there is a God of any kind.

A fourth assumption is that authentic science and religion are both at base a quest to understand the same reality. Although it is almost universally taken for granted that science and religion pursue two different realities, I would assume that reality of its very nature must be one – there cannot be two realities - and authentic science and authentic religion work in awareness of this. Cosmology and quantum science have taken us up to, and into, what I have elsewhere called "the physics of ultimate reality"[2] and for that very reason must be of interest to the religionist who feels a deep need to know more about the ultimately reality, the creating power that is traditionally known as God. That such a power exists is, of course, a proposition that raises the most violent controversy, and all I would say in this introduction is two things: firstly, many of the world's greatest and most pioneering scientists have found sufficient evidence to believe that it does exist and to conduct their lives on the basis of that belief, and it would be rash to conclude that they were all deluded chumps. Secondly, the proper attitude for any individual, scientist or not, who feels no sense of an unknown higher power is not to deny its existence but to adopt a position of open-minded agnosticism. More is said on this topic in the essays, "The Dawkins Phenomenon" and "Darwin contra Darwinism."

Let it be conceded that both science and religion are the quest to know more about different aspects of the same reality, and it is easy enough to appreciate that they approach it in complementary ways. These two approaches may be categorized, rather too simply, as from the outside and the inside. Science seeks understanding by observation and measurement, and religion by empathy, but both depend on acceptance of the same logic, and progress in both is dependent on what might be called intuitive leaps. Inspiration too is needed at critical points to take forward both science and religion. Temperamentally, the scientist and religionist may be drawn to understand reality from the outside or inside, the logical or the empathic, but awareness of that complementarity should make them respectful of each other, and grateful for each other's contribution to the truth, rather than antagonistic.

There are many organisations and journals which set out to show that science and religion are harmonious and even complementary, but these essays seek to justify a far more ambitious proposal, namely that the science and religion of the future will be symbiotic. This is of vital importance but needs to be tightly qualified, and qualification will call for a distinction between the philosophical and technical aspects of science, which I have labelled "philoscience" and "technoscience" in the essay "Beyond Einstein." My own bias, as a philosopher of evolution, will be apparent, but it is perhaps worth saying that I began my career as a mechanical engineer, and have a lively interest in the science-technology connection, and take deep enjoyment from it. *Pace* Wordsworth, earth has few things to show more beautiful than a Gresley locomotive or a Maillart bridge. The story of engineering from the Roman road to the Space Shuttle is a history of heroes.

What is needed most of all for progress in both science and religion is, I believe, simple honesty, the honesty of the child who is prepared to look at the evidence and see that, despite what authority is telling him, and despite the put-down he will receive for saying so, the emperor has no clothes. The Hans Christian Andersen tale is a parable that would grace the gospels, but the more we are embedded in any institution, scientific or religious, the harder it becomes to put its moral into practice. All sorts of subtle and not-so-subtle influences bear upon us to stand up not for truth simple but for what J. K. Galbraith called "institutional truth." Natural timidity, simple ignorance, professional ambition and the need to show solidarity with the group combine to blur any vision of truth that orthodoxy finds uncomfortable, and persuade us to look backward, rather forward. It is a paradox of science, often noted, that validation of new ideas through peer review is a highly effective mechanism for progress, except when fundamentally new ideas seek acceptance. In this case, as Max Planck wryly observed, science must wait until a generation of experts has died off.

As if this were not bad enough, when we encounter evidence that we do not wish to accept, a superior intellect will often find superior reasons for going into denial. While this accusation is routinely levelled against religion, it is often applicable to those who feel their scientific orthodoxy is under threat. As the evolutionary psychologist Stephen Pinker has put it, we often abuse the rational brain by turning it into a spin doctor, to keep intact our different belief systems - political, religious or scientific. The skill with which we are able to rationalise for any of these purposes may be illustrated in the following conversation, between a scientist and what might be called an educated flat-earther, which I adapt from John Barrow, making much the same point.[3] The two are discussing the nature of friction, with the flat-earther maintaining that a rolling ball is brought to halt by a horde of cunning little demons. The dialogue, if one can call it that, goes like this:

Scientist: *I don't see how demons can make friction.*
Flat-Earther: *They just stand in front of things and push to stop them from moving.*
Sc: *I don't see any demons even on the roughest table.*
F-E: *They are too small, and almost transparent.*
Sc: *But there is more friction on rough surfaces.*
F-E: *More demons.*
Sc: *But why does oil help to reduce friction?*
F-E: *It drowns the demons.*
Sc: *But I cannot feel these demons.*
F-E: *Just rub your finger along the table*

… and so on.

The point is, of course, that however ridiculous a hypothesis may be, most of us are capable of finding reasons for holding it, when our belief system is threatened.

The greater point I would like to make here is that neither science nor religion can make progress now without overcoming this defensive reflex. We are up against a problem here which is psychological, rather than rational, and which usually is sensed unconsciously as a threat to our identity. The wider point still is that since we have little ability to overcome this psychological barrier by rational debate, the only hope we have is through a process of education. Progress now depends on a commitment to transformative religion and a deeper understanding of the nobility of the scientific spirit. The most promising path to the future must lie, therefore, through historical and comparative studies which are the proper field of metascience and developmental theology. If this small work leaves the reader with a wish to know more, it will have succeeded in its purpose.

References

1. E. O. Wilson, *Consilience: The Unity of Knowledge.* NY: Little, Brown, 1999. p. 5
2. In *Jehovah and Hyperspace: Exploring the Future of Science, Religion and Society.* London: New European Publications, 2002.
3. John Barrow, *The Universe that Discovered Itself.* London: OUP, 2000. p. 54

Part 1:

AT THE CROSSROADS

The first essay in this part originated in half a dozen pages written informally for my wife some years ago. Over a period of several years it was amplified and photocopied on request, then printed as a booklet. The fact that it was positively received suggested that it was answering to a need, particularly of non-specialists, and hence worth including in the present work as an overview.

The next essay, on evolutionary biology, has been included as a counter to the widespread belief that evolutionary theory has pronounced the "death of religion," and is an answer to the arguments of Richard Dawkins.

The third essay, by contrast, puts forward a case for the "death of Christianity," if the term is taken to mean loyalty to certain historical beliefs that no reasonable person can accept today. The wider issue at stake is whether or not intellectual integrity is an essential element in authentic religion and spirituality.

RELIGION WITHOUT FAIRY TALES,
SCIENCE WITH SOUL

Two Revolutions, Two Revelations

The theologies of all established religions have been made obsolete by two scientific discoveries in the past one hundred and fifty years. Both concern evolution and both constitute revelation in the most literal sense, for they reveal something about the way our universe and we as human beings have been created. Thus they reveal something of critical importance about the creating power which we have traditionally called God.

Both discoveries are incomplete and thus, strictly, should be taken as theories rather than as facts, but the evidence that they are broadly correct is so overwhelming that they may be taken as factual truth. Both revelations have an immense bearing on the way we understand not only the creating power but the meaning of existence and the purpose of our own lives. Both are theologically dynamic, which is to say that in considering their significance we are led towards a change in the way we habitually feel, as well as think, and they initiate a change in our behaviour. Together these two scientific discoveries provide new theological energy, new incentive and capability, to attain the goal of what the early Christian church called *metanoia* – change of consciousness, change in the way we empathise, and change in the way we experience reality.

The importance of these scientific revelations cannot be over-stressed, for ultimately they must lead to a general awareness that the point of life is to develop into a new kind of human being, as different from what we now consider normal humanity as the normal human being today is different from our caveman ancestors. In this regard it is worth quoting from the social psychologist R. D. Laing, who wrote in 1967, after two "wars to end all wars" had made the stark truth unavoidable:

> *Normal men have killed probably a hundred million of their fellow normal men in the last fifty years.*[1]

The logical consequence of this is that unless we redefine what is meant by "normal human being", we shall never escape the mindless inhumanity that has caused such violence and loss of life. The new theology provides just such an escape: it offers salvation in the most literal sense. It is the introduction to a script for a new human future, and the prologue to a drama whose final act is the reinvention of the species. Those who would say that this is impossible, that human nature never changes, know nothing of our evolutionary history.

The first of these scientific/theological discoveries forcing us over a developmental barrier was Darwin's theory of biological evolution, which interpreted a range of evidence from nature and from the fossil record to show that species evolve, and the human species is part of this process. It is common to sum up Darwin's theory of human evolution in the snap phrase "Man came from monkeys", but the real significance of evolutionary theory comes not from looking back at what we once were but in looking forward to what we can be. As H. G. Wells put it a century ago:

> *The fact that man is not final is the great unmanageable, disturbing fact .... The question of what is to come after Homo sapiens is the most persistently fascinating and the most insoluble question in the whole world.*[2]

Darwin's scientific revelation forces us to make several theological decisions. Firstly, we must decide whether or not we believe that our species, and thus each individual, has further developmental potential and, secondly, unless the evidence leads us to believe that human evolution has suddenly and inexplicably come to an end, we must decide where it is tending. For millions of years our species evolved blindly, under pressure of its environment like other species, but now we know that we can purposely change our environment and our nature, and this freedom brings with it an awesome responsibility: it forces upon us the question, what kind of humanity do we want to bring into existence? It is increasingly said that we are co-creators, but rarely does anyone spell out what we are supposed to be creating. Now the question comes into sharp focus.

Various secular and religious ideals have been proposed in the past. Secular solutions have emphasized physical characteristics, such as Hitler's vision of a blond-haired Aryan master race, or high IQ or the individual dedicated to the state, such as the hard-working Stakhanovite of Soviet Communism. Religious solutions, by contrast, have emphasized a higher kind of consciousness, such as "the Buddha mind", "Krishna consciousness" and "the mind that was in Christ". Now we must ask are these religious concepts of the ideal human more or less equivalent and are they adequate to serve in the 21st century as models, or must we work out a new ideal, altering and adding to the old ones in order to take into account the fact that all the great spiritual leaders of the past lived in a vastly different kind of world and thus had a limited consciousness. If what Buddhists call "the monkey mind" is at one end of the human evolutionary spectrum, what are we to aim for at the other end as humankind's goal? Whatever we decide will shape our evolutionary future. A radically new answer will ultimately produce a radically new kind of human being.

The second great scientific revelation came unexpectedly from the discovery by the astronomer Edwin Hubble in the 1920's that distant galaxies were emitting a reddish light, the so-called "galactic redshift". This observation led ultimately to the conclusion that they were moving away from each other. The scientific logic which led to this conclusion is simple but not important here, for its significance arises from the wider conclusion that we live in an expanding universe. The revolution in scientific thinking which this discovery created is by no means yet over, and has not even begun in theology. It is all very new, so new, in fact, that Einstein's theories were originally based on the assumption that we live in a static universe composed of a single galaxy. Now we know that there are billions of other galaxies, all travelling away from each other at enormous speeds. Such is the enlarged and dynamic understanding of the universe that has come about within the last two generations.

The Crisis in Scientific Belief

The real revolution that Hubble set in train, however, becomes apparent when an imagined film of the expanding universe is wound back until we come to the first frame. Here there is scientific controversy which boils down to different acts of faith. On the one hand there are theorists who maintain that the universe began with a very small, but still finite, dense point of energy, a singularity, and on the other hand there are those who maintain that we must follow through the logic of "rewinding the film" to its end, which takes us to a seeming paradox, namely a point of no size, when, still winding our imaginary film, the whole vast cosmos disappeared like the last dot of light on the screen when we switch off the television. This leads us to ask, where it disappeared to, since this presumably is where it initially appeared from, and to ask how, and why? Such questions are disconcerting in the extreme to conventional scientists, who secretly wish they would go away. We do have a fingerhold on the problem, however, in the fact that this dimensionless point has its counterpart in normal physics, which lives quite comfortably with the idea, and the reality, of a point charge on a smaller scale.

It is probably fair to say that belief in a cosmos which began as an immense point charge is not attractive to most physicists because it poses the seemingly theological question of where and how the point itself originated. Further, it represents a silent threat to conventional science, which is not equipped to deal either with infinities or "non-objects" that have no size, and hence there is fear among scientists that to go further in exploring this new territory will lead straight back into the religion from which science escaped four centuries ago, with all its superstitions and authoritarianism. The agnostic scientist Robert Jastrow graphically expressed this fear in his 1978 book *God and the Astronomers*:

> *Theologians generally are delighted with the proof that the Universe had a beginning, but astronomers are curiously upset. .... It turns out that the scientist behaves the way the rest of us do when our beliefs are in conflict with the evidence. We become irritated, we pretend the conflict does not exist, or we paper it over with meaningless phrases .... For the scientist who has lived by his faith in the power of reason, the story [of modern cosmology] ends like a bad dream. He has scaled the mountains of ignorance, he is about to conquer the highest peak; as he pulls himself over the final rock, he is greeted by a band of theologians who have been sitting there for centuries.*[3]

What the scientists have found has become a subject of lively debate, with a tacit division along theological lines between those whose logic forces them to regard the Big Bang as an event which brought our three-dimensional world into existence from some prior reality and those whose logic equally prevents them from accepting the existence of any other kind of reality than the familiar world of our senses. Since it is almost universally assumed that time began at the moment of the Big Bang, and widely assumed that any "prior reality" must be higher dimensioned, probably infinitely dimensioned, it is not surprising that an emerging new science which deals with the timeless and infinite seems to many to be a contradiction in terms. Whereas mystics associate infinity with perfection, philosophers are usually nervous about it because the idea is difficult to grasp. Rudy Rucker notes in his *Infinity and the Mind* that the Greek word for infinity, *apeiron* (without limit) was also used to describe things without order, such as "a crooked line [or] a dirty crumpled handkerchief."[4] Those physicists today who are drawn to go beyond the Big Bang in search of its origins find themselves leaving the conventional domain of solid reality to enter into the unobservable domain of mathematical infinity, where experimental proof is impossible.

Although belief in the infinite and unseen may at first seem irrational, it is, in fact, directly comparable to the step which the child takes into mental maturity when it starts to believe in the existence of what it does not immediately see. The Swiss psychologist and educator Jean Piaget first drew attention to the significance of this developmental stage. When a small baby is shown an object which is then hidden behind a screen or the experimenter's back, it will lose interest, for as far as it is concerned the object no longer exists. A few months later, however, it will show delight in its discovery that the object continues to exist, and in the proof that is given when it is brought again into view, a delight shared by every parent as they play this game. Such is the surprise and delight, at a higher level, that comes from realising that "the world invisible" of science does not lose its reality simply because we cannot observe it with our limited human senses. Physics and cosmology are now at a critical threshold where what St Paul called "faith in things unseen" has become as important in science as in religion. What is vital in both cases, in order to distinguish such faith from gullibility, is to know the rational grounds for holding it and for building a science and religion upon it.

Scientific believers and non-believers both agree that the Big Bang, whether a small point or a true dimensionless point, consists of electromagnetic energy in an unimaginably dense state. This energy is made up ultimately of the same particles of light, the photons, which not only enable us to see the world around us but make up the electrons, and thus the atoms of which we are composed. Again the disputed question rises as to whether the photon of light is very small in size or is a point of energy without dimension, which normally travels on a wavelike path. If the latter stand is taken, the Big Bang can be understood as originating in a single "superphoton", containing all the photons in the universe compressed, as it were, into one dimensionless point. In fact, the event we usually call the Big Bang, or sometimes the Hot Big Bang, is referred to by some astronomers as the "Big Flash". Whichever term is used, it may be understood as the manifestation in three-dimensional space of a higher energy in a higher dimension. The consequence of this logic seems to be that there exists a higher source of energy beyond human sense, which is the origin of everything in our universe. Such a "light beyond light" calls to mind the God of traditional theology, and it is this possibility which raises in agnostic scientists, and indeed in religiously minded scientists too, the genuine fear that to seek to know what caused the Big Bang will ultimately dissolve the integrity of science.

Speculation so rarified threatens to be unprovable and hardly more than superstition.

Scientific and Theological Creeds: Dividing the Garment of Truth

The great act of faith that scientists make today is a matter of negative belief that we cannot know how the Big Bang happened, but the great act of faith of "religionists" is also negative, that spiritual truth can only be conveyed through myth, legend, allegory and – let us be blunt – fairy story. In practice science and religion have agreed to partition truth into two territories, with observable and measurable truth being handed over to science and mythological truth to religion. The late palaeontologist Stephen Jay Gould formulated this as a principle, which he called, rather grandly, "Non-overlapping Magisteria of Authority" (or NOMA for short), meaning that science and religion could pursue their own kind of truth and need never interact. In fact, this was proposed eight centuries ago by the Moslem philosopher Averroes, who called it the Principle of the Double Truth. His followers, including many so-called Christian Averroists, held that it was allowable (and ethical) to hold a religious truth in the religious compartment of one's mind, so to speak, and a contradictory truth in the scientific compartment. History is now repeating itself, for the great example then was the same as it is today, whether the universe had existed forever, as Aristotle had taught, or had been created in time, as the Bible and the Koran teach.

Many philosophers seized with relief on this get-out principle of two different but equally valid answers, for it apparently solved an insoluble problem of conscience. One outstanding theologian, however, led the movement against it. Thomas Aquinas insisted that truth could not be divided in this way, and wrote his monumental *Summa Theologica* around 1250 to make his point. Far from applauding his genius, the religious authorities on the whole were suspicious, and the archbishop of Paris went so far as to publicly burn Aquinas's books for trying to mix religion with the science of the day. In the end, however, the principle of the oneness of truth prevailed in the West, with the direct consequence that Islamic science and religion, which adopted the Principle of the Double Truth, both declined as world forces, while western science soon started to forge ahead. There is a great moral there for those who think we can have a healthy, and health-giving, science and religion by insulating each of them from the awkward questions that arise where their domains of enquiry overlap.

Although science and religion are both concerned with truth, it is a sad fact that we rarely see them this way, for both are compromised. Science's honesty is dispensable as it becomes too closely associated with technological advance, big business and profit-making, and every religion's honesty becomes subordinated to propagating the particular myth on which it is based. As the economist J. K. Galbraith put it, truth simple loses out to institutional truth. Religious leaders do not feel a primary responsibility to honesty and openness in matters of truth, for their calling is to hand on a "deposit of faith" in which truth is defined unquestionably in terms of foundational myths, laid down in all cases in a pre-scientific age. Although minor myths can be reinterpreted, questioning the great original myths is not allowed, it is heresy. All this is not to deny that spiritual understanding can be communicated through non-factual, essentially poetic, means, for if this were not so, it would be hard to explain how civilization has evolved. Nevertheless, the unwillingness of all mainstream religions to question, let alone abandon, their founding myths represents a kind of universal denialism. It can be confidently predicted that, whatever their present differences, the world's religions, which are now in opposition to each other, will find common cause and an unexpected solidarity when a new kind of religion makes its claims, based on what has been called "the epiphany of science."

Truth, Conscience and Flat-earth Theologies

Since all the major religions are theories of reality that were proposed before we knew that we lived on a round earth, it is not inaccurate to say that they are based quite literally on flat earth theologies. As a consequence, the truth-seeker today is forced to reject religion in order to retain his or her intellectual integrity or else to silently refuse assent to the items of belief that offend their conscience. Many hang on in this way. There are sincere Jews who do not believe that a God above the clouds gave the land of Palestine to the tribe of Hebrews in perpetuity and ordered the slaughter of its original inhabitants, Catholics who do not believe that they eat the flesh and drink the blood of a God-man called Jesus every Sunday, Protestants who do not believe that the same person magically resuscitated his own corpse three days after death and then went back to a heaven above the clouds, Hindus who doubt that the cow is a specially sacred animal, though there is probably no practising Moslem who does not believe that all truth now and forever is revealed somewhere in the Koran. On that act of faith hinges both the strength and weakness of Islam, and so too with all religions based on closed-end revelation. Religion, like all else human, evolves, not only by incremental changes but by periodic revolutions when the grandeur of new revelation demands a re-laying of foundations. In the rear-view mirror of history our descendents will come to see that the early twenty first century marked the clear beginning of just such an epochal change.

The mythological differences between so-called faith communities, would be a matter for smiles at human weakness, were it not for the fact that the world is likely to destroy itself as the cultural blocs which have grown out of the world's great religious myths come into nuclear conflict. Those who wish to harmonise religious myth and scientific discovery tend only to spin pseudo-scientific fantasy from ancient myth. Matthew Fox, for instance, the well known rebel Catholic priest and eco-theologian, redefines the Eucharist as "our eating and drinking of the Cosmic Christ".[5] What this might mean to a spiritual seeker with an Islamic or Buddhist background, or indeed any normal person, is by no means clear, but it must surely erect an insuperable barrier in any movement to bring the world's spiritual seekers together. The example simplifies an argument that has many dimensions of complexity, but the fact remains that until humankind is able to construct a theory of ultimate reality that goes beyond all these primitive theologies and their modern elaborations, there is no hope for permanent peace in the world. The religious decisions we must now make may be compared metaphorically to those which face peasants living on the slopes of a volcano that has grumbled for centuries and caused periodical damage but which now is erupting on a vaster scale and pouring out lava in greater quantities. To leave their familiar houses and the land they own and strike out into the unknown is unthinkable for most, and talking together in crisis meetings, they are able to convince each other that the approaching lava will probably stop and life could then resume as normal. A few, however, are clear-sighted enough to see that this act of faith goes against the evidence, and on these few the future will depend. Their conviction is that if they do not act radically, exile themselves and go into to the unknown, there will be no future.

New Horizons in Science

It would be far too simple to say that we only need a "scientific" theology to resolve the religious crisis, if only because the foundations of science are themselves being shaken, and the rebuilding of science on new principles is becoming urgent. It will be a science of being (ontology) and of knowing (epistemology), for science is now asking radical questions about how reality is to be defined and recognized, how we know and how we can be certain. A new kind of science is being forced upon us because quantum physics has to deal with patterns of energy, not the "hard, solid, massy, unbreakable" particles of Isaac Newton's science, and, strange as it may seem, scientists have no clear idea of what energy actually is, only of its physical effects. We need to know now what is the reality that underlies chemical, electrical, magnetic, heat and light energy and how these are related to the energy of motion. What is it that remains invariant in all the transformations of energy? Is the energy of consciousness part of this rich tapestry? We are in no doubt that the willed intention to lift our arm, for instance, is sufficient to set a train of muscular events in motion, and there have been rigorous experiments which have shown that the willed intention of humans and even animals can influence external events on a small scale. The great scientific bogey which rattles its chains behind a curtain of denial is the question of whether a greater consciousness can influence things on a larger scale. In principle it is possible, but as things stand at present, religion says it happens and science says, in effect, that it cannot happen. A neutral observer would have to say at least that both convictions cannot be right.

In its early period science as we know it was called natural philosophy: today it could be called "unnatural philosophy", for at the frontier it probes into a higher dimensioned reality within which our ordinary 3D world is contained, rather perhaps dissolved like salt in brine or water in wine. This metaphor can, in fact, be formalized mathematically using the discipline of topology, but the mental image is not a bad place to start, and is quite adequate for the non-mathematical seeker.

Science's new perception of reality in which our three-dimensional expanding cosmos is in some way contained in a higher dimensioned universe may seem at first difficult to understand. This is partly because it is unfamiliar and partly because it is impossible to visualize. Lack of familiarity is no more a permanent obstacle than was the difficulty our recent ancestors once experienced in understanding how the earth can go round the sun when we can see the sun going round the earth each day. As regards visualisation of a reality with more than three dimensions, we are very limited by our sense of sight and particularly by the fact that illustrations on the page must be reduced to two-dimensional models. Nevertheless, we can gain a fingerhold on what is at issue by the following figure, which the labels make more or less self-explanatory. Before the Big Bang point the diagram shows a small triangle labelled "Planck domain". This is an unimaginably small area, billionths of billionths smaller than a speck of flour, which came into existence billionths of a second after the Big Bang, and it marks the boundary of science's present knowledge. Physicists have no idea of the "structure" of energy during this period of expansion, and this is why they tend to draw a line here in their theorizing.

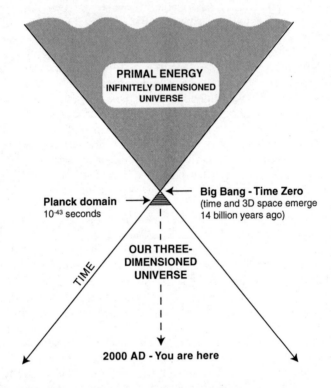

Fig 1 The emergence of our universe of space and time

Fig. 1 shows the cosmos at the start of its evolution, and Fig. 2, a *jeu d'esprit* of the eminent physicist John Wheeler, shows its current stage. It illustrates how the emergence of humanity has given consciousness to the universe - represented as the large "U".

Fig 2. The universe becomes self-conscious

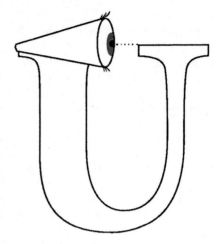

Both these diagrams can be contrasted with the following, which is a representation of a world view from two thousand years ago. It is a composite made up from different statements about the nature of heaven and earth in the Old and New Testaments.

Fig. 3 The biblical world view

Odd as it may appear to the modern mind, it is by no means illogical, for if the rain comes down from above, it is not unreasonable to hypothesize the existence of a firmament of water between heaven and earth. This would have been the world view of Jesus and his contemporaries, thus making the story of his bodily ascent into heaven through a cloud - which conveniently "removed him from the disciples' sight" (Acts 1:9) perfectly believable. The Greek "scientific" model of the cosmos, it is worth noting, was quite different from this commonsense world view, locating the earth at the centre of revolving crystal spheres which carried the stars.

Although the crisis in science may not seem to be of interest to the non-scientist, it is in fact of vital importance to all of us, for it brings into question the scientific attitude, and this is a high moral principle which, if abandoned, would set back human development disastrously. Imagine, for instance, the effect on medical science if disease was attributed to evil spirits, as Jesus seems to have assumed, or what confidence would we have in the TV weather girl if she forecast thunder and put it down to an irritable god making its presence felt. Without thinking too much about it, we assume the need for a level of factual truth and a logic of cause-and-effect in almost all aspects of our life today which was not the case in the childhood of the human species. This demand for factual and historical truth is a direct result of the way in which the objective standards of science have become part and parcel of our normal awareness. When it comes to religion, however, we tend to accept much that it is childishly naive simply because it has been handed down to us in that particular form.

The Crisis of Truth in Christianity

The problem of science versus religion would be easier if scientific issues did not overlap and conflict in many places with religious belief. This overlap is unavoidable, for both are based on theories of reality and, presumably, there is ultimately only a single reality – that's what makes it really real! Although science clashes with all the world's religions - except those which have no interest at all in factual truth - it clashes most profoundly with Christianity, firstly because Christianity claims to be based on historical fact, not legend, and because it has formed the basis of Western civilization. When the objective truth of the Christian myth comes under fundamental questioning, the superstructure of our culture starts to rock - from sexual mores to family structure, from standards of justice to political and commercial values.

One example of the overlap between religion and science which has profound consequences for self-understanding is the conflict between the Bible story of Adam and evolutionary history. We can interpret much of the Bible and the ancient scriptures of other religions to harmonise them with modern knowledge, as, for instance, the *Genesis* account of how the world was created in six stages matches remarkably well with the evolutionary sequence revealed by science. We cannot, however, reinterpret the story of Adam's fall in this way, because on its assumed historical truth rests a vast and interlocked structure of doctrine and religious practice. Most importantly, the story of Adam and Eve, which was astonishingly insightful when first created, leads to a particular definition of man which has put a ceiling on our evolutionary potential. From the logic of Original Sin has emerged the necessity for baptism to remove it and a schizophrenic theology which on the one hand emphasizes our innate sinfulness but on the other assures us that we are kin with the sinless Jesus, who is, in the words of St Paul, "the first born of a great new human family". Rephrased in terms of modern biology, Paul is saying that he understood Jesus to be the holotype of a new kind of human being, the term holotype being given to the first discovered specimen of a new genus, species or subspecies of plant or animal. For lack of an evolutionary sense, however, mainline Christianity cannot convince people of their untapped potential for love, but is forced instead to stress inherited guilt in order to justify the saving virtue of a self-sacrificial God-man. Thus has the core myth of Christianity of all denominations choked the seed of evolutionary optimism that is there in plain scriptural view if we wish to find it.

The theory of Jesus the sacrificed saviour has become the very keystone of classical Christianity, and not just as an allegory or metaphor: belief in its literal truth is explicit, as for example in the preamble to the eucharistic prayer of the Church of England:

> *Almighty God, our heavenly father, who of thy tender mercy didst give thine only son Jesus Christ to suffer death upon the Cross for our redemption, who made there (by his one oblation of himself once offered) a full, perfect and sufficient sacrifice, oblation and satisfaction for the sins of the whole world ....*

The same sentiments are found just as explicitly in the Roman Catholic Mass and in most Protestant worship, and they cannot be dismissed as antiquated expressions of a more subtle theology. The 1976 publication *Christian Worship*, a cooperative work of Baptists, Methodists and United Reform Church which was purposely written as an updating of "the eternal verities of God's revelation in Christ" finds nothing remarkable about including William Cowper's 18th century composition:

> *There is a fountain filled with blood*
> *Drawn from Immanuel's veins;*
> *And sinners plunged beneath that flood*
> *Lose all their guilty stains ....*

The compilers express the modest hope that hymns like this are examples of "good poetry and good theology."

In a pre-scientific age such theology was acceptable and believable, but today if Christians were honest about what they really believed, most would have to preface the Creed, as they recite it each Sunday, with "This I don't believe". Instead, they metaphorically cross their fingers behind their backs when it comes to things that conflict with the logic of their ordinary world view, such as the virginal conception of Jesus and his departure from this earth by levitation to a far off realm where his living body continues to exist. A generation which has seen astronauts in space on television and distant galaxies captured by the Hubble telescope cannot take seriously a God-man rising, like Elijah in his chariot of fire, to a mythical heaven above the clouds. The split world view of Christian theology creates a credal and constitutional dishonesty which runs throughout the churches and drains them of spiritual power. It cannot be put right by tweaking doctrines here and there. We are entering now into a second Axial Age which, like the first will be marked by a fundamentally new understanding of what we mean by "God" and by the changes in religious practice that will follow.

A New Axial Age

In the first Axial Age, which occurred over a period of several centuries around 500 BC, the world moved slowly from belief in many gods, goddesses and godlets invented at will to belief in a single external power. Judaism stood out from the new religions for several reasons, most notably because the Jews insisted on the need for an objectively real divinity who was "holy"; that is to say, a God who reflected the finest human qualities. Now a new kind of religion is being born from the knowledge that science is bringing. It is to be expected that those who have a vested interest in religion in its current form will resist new theological inspiration, for we all resist major change almost instinctively. Not only do we fear the mental disturbance that will accompany it, but we have a genuine reason to hold back, since we do not know in advance that the new will prove any more effective than the old.

A new kind of religion is like a newly designed plane: until it is airborne, no one can be sure that it will reach its declared destination, or even that it will fly, and no one can be too critical therefore of those who decline to get on board. From what has been already said it will be clear that if there is to be an evolutionary surge to a higher level of spiritual awareness, a new religion will need to have several qualities, the first of which will be honesty. It might be objected that such things as love and humility are more basic, but this would be to miss the point that the newness rests in not in the spiritual experience itself, which many individuals have had throughout the ages, but in honest acceptance of a new world view which will provide an intellectual path. That in itself will not take us to the experience of oneness – though it may possibly do so for some philosophically minded souls – but it is one way to the gate, where the decision to enter must be made. Instead of trying to understand religious realities as our ancestors understood them nearly two thousand years ago, we must reframe our finest spiritual intuitions to match up with the way in which we understand a world revealed by science. Simple honesty is an essential requirement, not just an option, because the grip of the old can only be loosened by bringing to the authority of age-old doctrines the same eyes that look out on a world transformed by technology and by economic and political change. For some it will take courage to question received religion but those for whom openness of mind is an instinctive value – like the child who told the experts that the emperor had no clothes – all that will be required is the application of ordinary standards of truth. Those who feel that religion is not necessarily connected to personal honesty and intellectual integrity will see no need to change.

The second condition for a new religion is that in generating new awareness of the power we call God it creates in us a new sense of self - that is to say, a new awareness of who we are. It is common today to promote a religion-free spirituality, but little reflection is needed to see that our sense of who we are is critically dependent on the community in which we grow up. From it we take our values, great and small, almost every aspect of our behaviour, our moral code and everything that we consider normal. Even the way we use a knife and fork to eat is something we have learned in the process of "socialisation". We may choose as adults to diverge from some of these values, but what we consider our very individual self is mostly a reflection of the world view imposed on us from birth by family, school and national community. To take a simple but striking example, if we had been placed when a few weeks old into a cannibal community (such as existed until recently in the New Guinea highlands), by the age of ten we would have taken cannibalism as normal, along with many other modes of thought and behaviour, and we would have a quite different kind of intelligence and sense of self.

From this line of argument it becomes clear that what faces us now is the construction of a higher kind of community which will enable us to grow into a different kind of human being with a different understanding of what is "normal". St Paul said of his vision of Christianity that "there is no longer Jew and Greek, freeman and slave, male and female" (*Galatians 3:28*), but we are looking now at a future where this vision expands critically, to a world where there is no longer American or Chinese, Moslem or Christian, straight or gay. What over-rides all these "natural" distinctions which seem so essential to my sense of self is the common awareness that my true self is "that of God within", the "Overself". If we are convinced by science that every atom in our body has its origin in the primal energy which we call God, we shall find it much easier to take that leap of awareness which once was considered to be the incomprehensible preserve of a few mystics in every age.

A third quality and necessary condition for a genuinely new religion follows from what has just been said, that the religious community must be global. We can no longer be satisfied with tribal, national or continental religion, nor with any which calls itself universal but whose mindset was formed in the days most of the known world was included within the Roman or Arabic empires. A global religion will call for a revolution in the thinking of most people, who take for granted that the religio-cultural blocs into which the world is now divided are in some way "natural" and permanent. This is the blind spot which afflicts even the most liberal theologians and church-men and women. The chief rabbi of Britain, Jonathan Sacks, without doubt spoke for all religious leaders when he recently wrote of ecumenism that while mutual friendship is desirable, and it is true that there is one God and one humanity, such truths must not blind us to the fact of life "that each great faith is a universe."[6] The contradiction in the word "universe" as he uses it goes unnoticed, but it would surely be more accurate to say that each great faith believes and acts as if it were a universe, and that is where some of the world's most grievous ills begin.

A true and honest universe of religion must transcend all present day divisions, and to do this it will require a coherent theology which not only appeals to head and heart but makes them resonate together and amplifies their spiritual energy in unison. Its construction will require new learning structures and materials, processes of interaction and modes of authority, purpose-designed meeting places and liturgy to fit a new purpose. That purpose is to build what has never existed since our ancestors were all hunters, namely a global religious consciousness, a worldwide community not limited to a sense of oneness with nature but bonded by the common quest for the experience of oneness with the reality which is our source and the source of nature.

As the German theologian Dorothee Sölle has said, "Religion in the third millennium will either be mystical or dead."

There is more than one definition of mysticism, but whatever meaning is chosen, it is something different from what the average person expects ordinary religion to offer. Yet this is the great challenge of a global family, not to bring together those who seek in religion a vague "spiritual" comfort but those who seek to fulfil their human potential by developing an habitual sense of oneness with the divine. This is the doctrine that all the great religious teachers, from Shankara in Hinduism, Jesus in Judaism and Rumi in Islam (to name but three) have preached and for which many have been persecuted and even killed by the religious leaders of their time. It does not set itself against nature "to rule over every living thing that moves upon the earth", as in the Book of Genesis, but sees divinity in the natural world. It recognizes the infinite in the particular, each element manifesting the power of its creator. In Eckhart's words,

> *The most trivial thing **perceived in God**, a flower for example as espied in God, would be a thing more perfect than the universe.*[7]

The phrase "perceived in God" is the key, it is an unnatural mode of consciousness for humans at their present stage of evolution, and developing it, I would argue, is the task of true religion today. What the phrase means may be appreciated by reading spiritual poetry from all religious traditions and all ages. Some idea of its significance may be obtained by contrasting it with the everyday theology of the Christian Middle Ages. The emphasis then was on seeing things *sub specie aeternitatis,* that is to say, habitually aware of the shortness of this life in relation to the eternity of the next.

Science's story of creation is only narrative theology brought up to date, but it differs from the myths and legends of the past in two vitally important ways. Firstly, it deals with historical fact and rational hypothesis, and, secondly, it is a dynamic and inspirational story - it reveals both a new challenge and the way forward. A theology which takes us to the Big Bang and beyond will carry us out of time and into the timeless and infinite. It will take the restless searching which identifies the human species to a higher level, seeking the experience of the timeless in what the spiritual master de Caussade called so strikingly "the sacrament of the present moment," and what T. S. Eliot described no less strikingly in his *Four Quartets:*

> *Man's curiosity searches past and future*
> *And clings to that dimension. But to apprehend*

> *The point of intersection of the timeless*
> *With time, is an occupation for the saint.*[8]

Finding the Guides

Where are the leaders into the future to be found? The instinctive reaction of most people will be to look to existing religious leaders, but this would be as logical as putting Colonel Sanders in charge of chicken welfare, for, as has been argued, their vision is an inheritance from the past and their concept of leadership is modelled at best on the shepherd and the flock of dependent sheep and at worst on a self-perpetuating and largely unelected priestly authority. Scandals of paedophile priests in recent years have uncovered a wider scandal of institutional corruption in the way they have been protected by their superiors, the "leaders" of the church, and allowed to continue their predation. The abuse of executive power in democratic politics is widely reported, but nowhere is such abuse so blatant as in the unaccountable leadership of certain religious bodies. New wine, as Jesus said, needs new wineskins, and a global, post-mythological religion which seeks the experience of oneness with the creating power is very definitely a new wine. A new concept of religious leadership will be called for by a new concept of religion, where mutual help rather than top-down authority will be of the essence. A new type of teacher will emerge from those who are themselves on the new path but can offer guidance to others less advanced or less spiritually gifted. Paradoxical as it may seem, the new leaders will be those who are most acutely aware that they themselves are, and always will be, learners. A richly embroidered cloak, imposing tall hat and mace of office are totally inappropriate symbols of the kind of spiritual leadership for which the Western world is now calling.

The new religion cannot develop within a structure of gurus and devotees but only of co-learners and co-teachers. Together they will form a community extended in geographical space by global communication technology but closely bound locally, a community in which individualism is cherished, in which self-learning and self-discipline will combine with mutual support and guidance, and where leadership, though vitally important, is only one of the gifts which is held at the service of the community. This is not different in spirit from the way that the primitive Christian church was organised, and which may serve as an example. The love and sense of mutual dependence which energized its birth and growth are as essential a requirement now as then. In our individualistic age the need for unselfish service calls for particular emphasis if we are to have any hope of attaining the ideal of community, which Bishop John Vincent Taylor described beautifully in his book *The Go-Between God*:

> *Like a peal of bells the word* **allelon** *– 'one another' - rings through the [Greek] New Testament. Accept one another,. serve one another, wash one another's feet, confess your sins to one another, and pray for one another, comfort one another and build each other up, bear one another's burdens, love one another as I have loved you.*[9]

In a true religious community we are to be, as St Paul described it,

> *servants to one another in love (Gal. 5:13)*

an ideal of mutual service which runs throughout the documents of the early Christian church as a prime imperative:

> *Above all, hold unfailingly your love for one another, since love covers a multitude of sins. Practice hospitality ungrudgingly to one another. As each has received a gift, employ it for one another. (Peter 4:7-9)*

The emphasis here on loving service may be contrasted with the ideal of spirituality that characterizes our socially atomized age and which is sometimes given the umbrella labels of "New Ageism" or mind-body-spirit. Although the terms cover many kinds of belief and activity, it is probably true to say of most forms that they over-emphasize the individual at the expense of community, the occult over the rational and a misty romantic past over an intellectually inspiring future. In such a context, there is a real danger that the search for "spirituality" can become a refined form of self-indulgence, "getting blissed out" as the follower of an Eastern guru once described to me his spiritual ambition.

Making the Vision a Reality

As the parable of belling the cat tells us, there is not much point in having inspirational ideas unless there is logistical thinking to make them happen. Without a practical plan to get from here to there, we shall end with nothing but fine thoughts. Since the goal concerns attaining an habitual experience of oneness with the divine reality, the first step must be to establish connection as best we can with it through meditation, individually and in groups. This prescription is hedged with difficulties – what actually is meditation, what methods are to be used, how will we recognize the experience of oneness, is divinity to be found in the silence or is it the silence itself, do we seek or must we wait to be grasped? - as the beauty of a sunset grasps us - and so on. Such considerations, important as they are, must be passed over here, since the theme of this argument is essentially theological. The absolute and necessary starting point is quite simple: we must ask the power which created us and infuses every cell in our body to reveal what needs to be done and put ourselves at its disposal. All who come together in the quest have a permanent listening role, and some will be natural followers, but none must follow passively like sheep, for all will have, in their own degree, a teaching role to play. All must be heard with discernment, for we do not know in advance where wisdom will be revealed. While it is common enough today to dismiss the naive concept of divinity as a nebulous male entity in the sky, we do not yet have a robust model to replace it. This is a critical weakness, for our model of divinity is at the core of our theology and thus of our spiritual practice. Science points us towards a creating consciousness of which each one of us is, as it were, a holographic fragment, but this is no more than a suggestive thought, and it is hard to see at this point how it can be given the concreteness that a theological model requires. It can be said with confidence, however, that whatever may eventually emerge will need to co-exist for a long period with traditional concepts of God. To make use of a wise strategy used by spiritual guides in other contexts,[10] it is probably advisable to live with the model of a loving father God above the clouds as long as we can.

Inspiration may come from anyone, even "out of the mouths of babes and sucklings", as the Old Testament puts it, but in religion, as in science, it comes most reliably to the prepared mind. Preparation will therefore be an ongoing task that will involve listening, praying, reading, discussing, and reflecting. To start on the path we shall need to enlarge our understanding of what religion itself means by studying the history of religion in general and of specific religions. In this way we will come to understand more deeply the need for a new kind of religion, raise hidden questions, modify irrational enthusiasm, project a future path to avoid past mistakes and incorporate in the new what has proved to be valuable in the past.

On this foundation of knowledge of the past must be built the theology of the future, and all must engage in the common task of learning about science's account of creation. To those who associate religious truth with myth, this will doubtless seem an irrelevant demand and totally beyond the capacity and interest of ordinary non-scientific people. But this is not so, for science is telling us a marvellous story, as exciting as any tale of derring-do, as moving as any romance, as intriguing as any detective story. Science's story of creation may start as a "What happened?" but eventually becomes a "Whodunnit?" as the pieces fit together. The great unanswered question in science today is whether the cosmos is a closed or open system, and as the weight of evidence tips the balance towards an open system, science and theology find common ground and will eventually meet in an embrace as natural as that which has joined myth and theology in the past.

That is only half the new good news, however, for esoteric as all this frontier science may at first appear, it is perfectly capable of being presented in story form that can enthral an eight year old, and that is a task awaiting those story-tellers who know intuitively how children feel and understand. Such authors can turn their gifts into cash today (the author of the Harry Potter books is reputedly worth a quarter of a billion pounds), but the challenge here has a greater prize in store, nothing less than helping to create a global family by telling a global story that transcends all the tribal mythologies of the past. If the creation story of science is presented in the right way, the wonder of it will cross cultural boundaries, co-existing with other legendary histories until, without need for persuasion (let alone crusade or jihad) it comes to be the commonly accepted framework for understanding what it means to be human. The day when this has come about may be far into the future, but when it happens we shall have created a natural global bond to replace the tribal identities which have been generated until now by a multitude of particular mythologies and reinforced by different religions.

Just as all mainstream religions today are based on fictional creation stories from the past, the story of humankind's origins as we enter the third millennium must be that which science is telling us - there is no alternative - and it will be a critically unifying factor in a new kind of global family. As the ancient Greeks drew their identity from Homer's great saga of Ulysses, the Jews from Moses and the Exodus, the Americans from he War of Independence and the "winning of the West", a global community will create its identity from the freshly minted story of our cosmic and evolutionary origins and of the great men and women and heroic deeds of discovery and endurance which have taken our species upward step by step. The new global mythology will demand no more mathematics than one wishes to bring to it, and can be fitted to the needs and capacity of anyone with natural curiosity, from the brainiest adult to the child in primary school. The essence of the story can be compressed into the following graphic representation.

Fig 4 From Big Bang to Man the co-creator

All this is proposed before there is any programme or structure in existence, but at some future time a learning process will emerge that will help create the new consciousness through all the modes of intellectual and artistic experience. We in the West live today in a split world of culture, surrounded by the triviality, incoherence and brutalism of much modern art, poetry, music and architecture alongside the nostalgic relics of a bygone "age of faith". Lacking new inspiration, our first tendency is to try to revive the beauties of the past in isolation from the culture that produced them, but we cannot go back. A new source of inspiration is our only hope, and the purpose of this small book is to convince the reader that it is emerging into view, and it is the responsibility of each one of us to act as midwife. As the new revelation pervades common consciousness we may hope to see architecture and design as inspiring as the mediaeval cathedrals, the exuberant temple ornament of ancient Hinduism and the austere beauty of the symmetrical art of the mosque. We may expect new epics, on the scale of the *Mabharata* and Dante's *Divine*

Comedy, new art to rival Michaelangelo and Praxiteles, new music, as pure as Gregorian chant and Bach's cantatas and as rich and dramatic as Handel's *Messiah*. We may look forward to an updated version of Haydn's great oratorio *The Creation*, whose theme bursts forth with *"und es war Licht!"* – and there was Light. Cosmotheology tells the same story and with drama just as great.

Catch 23: The Cost of Becoming What We Are Not

After all the explaining, the discussion, planning and weighing up, the creation of a global family unified by religious inspiration will call for individual decision and ongoing, lifelong commitment thereafter. Without doubt, many who will find it intellectually appealing and even exciting will back off like the rich young man in Luke's gospel when it comes to sign-the-cheque time, and this will surely come, for the new sense of self is a "pearl of great price" which is only bought by progressive abandonment of the old. *Metanoia*, or self-transformation, is both a goal and a process, and the great difficulty in achieving it is that one must behave as if one possessed the new sense of self while one is in the first stages of seeking it. Thus there is inevitably a temptation to give up because it all seems so unreal, and this is why the support of a community whose members are all in the same boat is so vital.

From the individual's point of view, the new consciousness must co-exist for a long time with the old, and this uncomfortable and confused state can only be sustained by what might literally be called dedicated hypocrisy. This is not a facetious quip, but is at the heart of the problem of human evolution. Human nature has changed incrementally over long periods of time but every so often our species has crossed a barrier as it has diverged from its ape origins. We can, for instance, look back and see (with the advantage of a million years of hindsight) such evolutionary leaps happening as we learned to walk on two legs, as language evolved from instinctive grunts to syntactic communication, as we moved from hunting to agricultural societies, and so on. Each of these moves was psychologically disruptive and gave a new definition to "human nature". In the early part of each period of change there would be a great tendency to look back to what was familiar rather than press on into the unknown. Such evolutionary watersheds induced a kind of split consciousness which bordered on schizophrenia, a term that the psycho-historian Julian Jaynes used quite literally in his classic work, *The Origins of Consciousness in the Breakdown of the Bicameral Mind*. He was writing of perhaps the most disruptive of these periods, when our ancestors had to make the step from shared tribal consciousness, when each member thought and felt like the group and its leader, to becoming city dwellers, which was to lead to a sense of individualism and eventually to the social alienation which blights our age.

"Civilization," says Jaynes, "is the art of living in towns of such size that everyone does not know everyone else." [11] Today we in the West take this for granted and it requires a feat of imagination to even see urban living as an evolutionary challenge. It is, however, worthwhile reflecting on it, for our problem is almost a mirror image, how to go to a new kind of civilization and a new kind of consciousness by acquiring the art of living on a planet where national, linguistic and religious groups do not know each other and whose "natural" instinct is hostility towards the other. As man's survival once depended on moving from a hunting to an agricultural consciousness, which must have been a traumatic change, planetary survival now depends upon transcending the existing group-thinking of nation and religious faith from which we take our identity and acquiring a global consciousness. However long the quest may be, it can only come about by individuals making the decision to embark on the great adventure of changing their nature, and that is what I have called the Catch 23. The new seekers will often find themselves "between two worlds, powerless to be born", between a "real me" that they wish to transcend and a future "me" that has not yet been experienced.

In every personal odyssey there must be a long stretch when the individual will seem to be going against his or her "real" nature, when they must pretend to be generous knowing that they can be very mean, patient when their "natural" impulse is to act hastily, uncomplaining when they are champion whingers, empathic when they have little interest in how the other person, or group, actually feels, one with creation when "normally" they are not very aware of the beauty around them. Without experiencing the tension of these ambivalent feelings we cannot grow spiritually, and humankind cannot evolve.

From Science to the Religious Experience

Even though the new consciousness can only come when words have been left behind, we must try to capture it in words and concepts in order to communicate the challenge that humankind faces. A wordless argument is possible by re-running the "mental movie" of an expanding universe back to the point of creation, for then we become aware that everything that is in existence, and ever will be in existence in our cosmos, was once contained in the point of energy, where all the photons of light in the cosmos were once compressed and superposed in an initial state. This is the astrophysicist's version of the Bible's "In the beginning." Simple logic tells us that the pure energy at this point includes everything *in potentia*, like a seed that is later to grow into a plant with leaves, flower and fruit, as its hidden potential is manifested in time. How this seed of infinite light originated is a question for the future science of infinity and hyperspace. What is immediately important is that from a theological perspective the point of origin that we call the Big Bang included not only all the matter of the universe, from each atom to each galaxy, but all the consciousness which pervades the universe, from the smallest cell to the human being. It includes, therefore, the consciousness that is reading these words and that which is writing them.

One vitally important religious consequence of taking this perspective on reality is that traditional theology, which says that God created everything out of nothing, is shown to be not only wrong but upside down wrong. The doctrine of *creatio ex nihilo* is now seen to be a misleading fiction. All that exists and each one of us has emerged from the Ultimate Reality. We are, as it were, spun from God's own substance. By this logic everything in existence is made of God-stuff, but we humans are a very special case, because our self-consciousness can identify with divine consciousness. We too can create, though we seem to be more intent on destroying the planet with our present behaviour. It might be thought that in revealing that we are made of divine energy, cosmotheology will lead to conceit, but the opposite is, in fact, the case, for the most fundamental realisation which it brings is that God really is "all in all", and from this awareness comes an unselfconscious humility and what might be called an habitual attitude of prayer. The simple affirmation "that Thou art" is the great theological experience in words. In time, however, the words fade out, the pure awareness of divine reality takes over and eventually becomes a background against which all of life is understood and experienced.

This is what the best spiritual guides in all the world's theistic religions tell us and what they exemplify in their lives. What is new is that it is a rational conclusion which physical science is now forcing upon us, and it takes mystical theology from the margin to the centre of religion. No longer is a sense of oneness with divinity and with creation the exotic preserve of a few spiritually gifted individuals, for a mature scientific theology tends towards making mysticism the defining norm of religion. In bringing logical head and mystical heart into a harmony it creates a new kind of consciousness from their mutual resonance, and as this intensifies within the group, religion will take on a new vitality, change our lives, make us happy and capable of making others happy, and fill us with love that comes from the knowledge that we are an integral part of the Great Reality and co-creators with It. Properly understood, a post-mythical theology prepares us for an evolutionary challenge that could never before be imagined, the purposeful reinvention of the species. Human evolution has been a slow process – it has taken us perhaps three million years to go from *Homo erectus* to *Homo sapiens*, but we must move now to *Homo novus* with all deliberate speed, for time is no longer on our side.

References

1. R. D. Laing, *The Politics of Experience*. Penguin, 1967. p. 24

2. H.G. Wells, from a lecture to the Royal Institute, reported in *Nature* 65:326-331, 1902.

3. Robert Jastrow, *God and the Astronomers*. London: W & W Norton, 1992 [1978], p. 107

4. Rudy Rucker, *Infinity and the Mind*, Brighton: Harvester Press, 1982. p. 3. It is interesting that when Georg Cantor in the later 19th century created a revolutionary new way for mathematics to deal with infinities, it was dismissed by many of his peers as lunacy, and even the great mathematician Henri Poincaré, a most forward thinker in other respects, called it "a disease from which mathematics would soon recover". Within a generation, however, the equally great mathematician David Hilbert called Cantor's theory of infinity "a paradise from which no one shall expel us," a judgement which time has fully justified.

5. Matthew Fox, quoted in the foreword to John Punshon, *Encounter with Silence*. Quaker Home Service: London, 1994 [1987].

6. Jonathan Sacks, "Credo," *The Times*, October 12, 2002.

7. From Evans' translation of Eckhart's works, quoted in T. D. Suzuki, *Mysticism: Christian and Buddhist*, 1979 [1957]. p. 5.

8. From "The Dry Salvages", the third of the Four Quartets, p. 32 in the 1954 Faber edition.

9. John V. Taylor, *The Go-Between God*. London: SCM, 1972. p. 112.

10. George Fox, for instance, advised the young William Penn, wavering between religious commitment and aristocratic fashion, "Wear thy sword as long as thou canst," and Abbot Chapman similarly, having told a correspondent that silent prayer was the best kind, then advised her not to strive for it but to "pray with words as long as you can."

11. Julian Jaynes, *The Origins of Consciousness in the Breakdown of the Bicameral Mind*. Boston: Houghton Mifflin, 1976. p. 149. Published by Penguin in 1993.

THE DAWKINS PHENOMENON

The Phenomenon

Richard Dawkins' name must be known to almost everyone in Britain who has ever wondered who or what God is, or if such an entity exists. At the time of writing (August 2007) the Amazon top ten best sellers list includes no less than three of his books, plus one attempting to rebut his argument for atheism. His runaway best seller *The God Delusion*[1] has been for sale in piles near the checkout in my local supermarket, a position usually reserved for Harry Potter type works of fiction. Quotes in this paper will be from the paperback edition of *The God Delusion* unless otherwise attributed. The back cover blurbs, by respected critics such as Julian Barnes and Michael Frayn, pile up superlatives – "splendid, exhilarating, passionate, clever, uplifting, desperately needed, wonderful, joyous, magnificent, lucid, wise, makes me want to cheer." This is clearly more than publisher's hype, and one is forced to consider what new factors Dawkins has brought to the science-religion debate that would justify it.

That he has raised religious hackles is understandable - the title makes sure of that - but it is the kind of science that he preaches that raises my personal hackles most immediately. He wants to convert us to "science", a word I enquote because what he offers is a distorted, outdated and fatally flawed form of what I take to be science. If authentic science is agnostic when the facts are not known, Dawkins is not a role model, despite the fact that he is its semi-official spokesman, being the first holder of the Chair in the Public Understanding of Science at Oxford University.

Even in religion, where I place the highest value on honest agnosticism, Dawkins depreciates it: he will have nothing less than dogmatic atheism. In a section entitled "The Poverty of Agnosticism" he effectively rules it out as a valid position in the debate, on the grounds that the existence of God is less than fifty per cent probable. Given that he has used Zeus, Baal, Thor and the Flying Spaghetti Monster as God-equivalences, one can hardly refute his argument, but this example demonstrates a systemic weakness in his mode of argumentation. The quickness of his debating swordsmanship conceals the way in which he builds up his case by selecting the easiest targets and using them as straw men on which to exercise his powers of ridicule, while totally ignoring the strongest examples in favour of either religion or some entity that might legitimately be called God. It is all very well to accuse religion as being the cause of war – which it undoubtedly is – but it is also the cause of humanitarian work of many kinds, from soup kitchens to networks of hospitals. It was not atheists or humanists who were responsible for abolishing slavery, but a dedicated coalition of Anglican, Methodist and Quaker individuals. The historian Adam Hochschild wonders how any group could be so "roused to care about the rights of other people ... an ocean away. In all of human experience there was no precedent for such a campaign."[2] A balanced argument should include such information, as also at least a mention of the inhumanities perpetrated by atheists, such as Stalin, Pol Pot and Mao Tse Tung. These three between them have been responsible for more deaths than all the religious wars in history. However, Dawkins' undoubted debating skill, and his entertainment value, is very much dependent on the fact that he doesn't "do balance." This is not necessarily a totally negative criticism, for on really serious issues, when action is required, the emotional thrust of the argument is more important than philosophical detachment, and there is no doubt that Dawkins has thrown himself into perhaps the most serious issue of all, the evolution of the human species.

Some Areas of Agreement

Before arguing for a diametrically opposite approach to his, I must say that I agree with him on four fundamental things. His "New Ten Commandments" (p. 298) would be a good replacement for the Decalogue of the Old Testament, with some modification of his rather naïve absolutism. (Total lack of censorship, e.g., is an impossible ideal, if only because any editor must function as a censor.) As a practical guide to morality, it compares favourably with similar attempts to rewrite the original version and make it more appropriate to the needs of our time, rather than to those of a primitive nomadic tribe. Significantly, it focuses tightly on individual morality, and in this respect may be compared with Konrad Lorenz's new list of eight deadly sins: "overpopulation, destruction of environment, the decay of compassion and the cheapening of pleasure, the failure of parental training, the increased indoctrinability of the masses and the possession of nuclear weapons." [3]

I would also agree with him in ruling out Stephen Jay Gould's NOMA principle (non-overlapping magisteria of authority) as a compromise solution to the science-religion confrontation. However, while Dawkins sees Gould's live-and-let-live prescription as chickening out of a decision in favour of tough-minded atheistic science, my case rests on the assumption that in the end truth is one, and that history has proved the NOMA principle unworkable. It is an almost exact replication of the Double Truth Principle proposed by the Spanish Islamic philosopher Averroes (1126-98) to counter the same apparent discrepancy between scientific and religious truth. The key issue, then as now, was whether the world had existed from eternity, as Aristotle had taught, or had been created in time, as the Koran and the Bible taught. In effect, the Double Truth Principle allowed one to hold two contradictory beliefs, and Christian Averroism was eagerly adopted by many Western philosophers as a way out of their dilemma. It was largely due to Thomas Aquinas (1225-74) that the West rejected this convenient but schizoid view of truth. Moslem thinkers, by contrast, adopted Averroism under pressure from the religious authorities, and it is surely significant that from about this time Islamic science, which had been the pace-setter for four centuries, started to decline and Western science forged ahead.

A third point of agreement, which may seem to deliver me into Dawkins' hands, is that the days of mythological religion are over, or should be, but again there are qualifications to be made. Firstly, myth was a necessary vehicle of truth when scientific explanation was not available. Secondly, its importance continues, so long as most of the world's population remains illiterate and innumerate. That said, Dawkins is surely right in pointing up the deficiencies today of a religion based on belief that a male divinity above the clouds miraculously impregnated a virgin in Palestine, that this "son of God" self-sacrificed himself on a cross for the world's sins, and that his revived corpse walked the earth for forty days before ascending through the clouds back to his heavenly father. We can, and must, do better than that, but the psychological resistance to attempting it can never be underestimated.

The fourth point of agreement is Dawkins's assertion that "the human species is a threat to the human species."[4] The significance of this epigram is impossible to overemphasize but, again, while he sees the threat as coming from belief in God and what he calls elsewhere the "virus" of religion, I would see it as the challenge to establish a new kind of relationship with the creating power that science, especially cosmology, is now encountering. As a proponent of evolution, Dawkins is convinced that belief in God is blocking human progress, but there is another option which he does not consider, namely, that a rational belief in a non-mythological religion will give us the best of both worlds - scientific truth and spiritual awareness.

I would also go a long way to agreeing with Dawkins that religions operate as control structures, but there is fatal ambiguity here that afflicts many other areas of human experience, and not least the scientific community. Once any group develops a common aim, even so humble as forming a darts club, it needs an executive body, and this all too easily become a group with its own purposes, sometimes simply the exercise of power, which can subvert the original aims and very often does. Democracy is a prime example of this entropy of ideals, and in many respects has become what Lord Hailsham called "elective dictatorship." It is, therefore, not surprising that religion has spawned executive bodies which betray the original ideals. The suborning of science in a similar way seems to have escaped Dawkins' reforming eye, a point to be taken up later.

Areas of Disagreement

To come now to the main points of disagreement, Dawkins' dogmatic atheism is surely wrong-headed on two counts. Not only is cosmology providing new evidence for a creation event some fourteen billion years ago, and thus for a creating force of some kind, but the prior existence of a power that merits the term "god" is, to say the very least, not an implausible conclusion from the sheer fact of existence. I am a conscious being who exists – of this I can be sure – and since I did not create myself, my antecedents must contain the cause of my existence. What we have known for seventy years, but what neither scientists nor religionists previously knew, is that the causal chain of biological, physical and cosmological events goes back to the Big Bang. At this juncture science faces three critical questions: (1) How big was the Big Bang? (2) What caused it? and (3) the "hard problem": how did consciousness emerge from inorganic matter?

Regarding the first question, science is faced now with two clear, and mutually exclusive, alternatives, as it winds back the cosmological film to its beginning. Both are acts of faith, but one, I would submit, is more plausible than the other. We can stop the film where science as we know it is still able to cope, and premise that the Big Bang event was extremely small, but still finite, and if our primary aim is to keep conventional science intact, this is logically acceptable. Alternatively, if we allow for the emergence of a new scientific paradigm, we can take a deep breath and go all the way. If genuine science is about the pursuit of truth, and hang the consequences, we must surely go all the way to a naked singularity, a mathematical point of no dimensions that existed in some unclear sense "before" time, or space, had come into being. Most physicists draw back from this, not only because they simply have no idea how to handle things which are not *res extensa*, but also, as Roger Penrose and others have argued, because such a dimensionless point implies an infinity of energy. Neither classical nor quantum physics can handle infinities,[5] but there is, in fact, no reason why a finite cosmos should have originated in a point of infinite energy, except the need to keep Einstein's General Relativity intact. This over-riding consideration has affected the mathematical reasoning. A thermodynamic approach to the cosmos would lead to a simpler conclusion: in a closed system energy content remains constant, so a finite cosmos would have begun with an immense but finite density of energy.

Although Dawkins' crusade is not concerned with this particular issue, it is worth noting that Einstein's theory was put together to explain the origin of the gravitational force before cosmology as such existed, when we did not even know that there was any other galaxy than our own It assumes a static universe, for it came out twelve years before Hubble provided the evidence for an expanding cosmos. Faced with the question of origins, which has fundamental significance for both science and theology, Dawkins resorts to hand-waving. When asked what was "in the beginning", he replied, without further elaboration but great authority, "Simplicity." [6] Such a reply is no more informative than answering "Magic." Given that science is now aware that consciousness is a form of energy, and takes it for granted in brain-scanning technology, it is perfectly logical to posit that the triggering event that set the cosmos expanding was an act of conscious will. However hard mainstream scientists may need to grit their teeth to admit it, this is not only a plausible alternative to the un-caused causes of "chance and necessity" and "quantum fluctuations" but is a far more plausible explanation. T. H. Huxley famously said that the great tragedy of science is its willingness to let an ugly fact wreck a beautiful theory, but this is also its greatest nobility and the challenge which gives it moral superiority, and it is an ugly fact that the train of electro-chemical events which result in my lifting a mug of tea is triggered not by a physical cause but by an act of intelligent will. Without such a willed intention nothing will happen.

At the very least, therefore, we cannot rule out that the cosmos began as an act of a cosmic, or extra-cosmic, will of some unknown kind, a reality beyond our normal ken. I would take it as a scientific principle that the "God of the gaps" should be resisted as long as possible, since it is a causal explanation that does not explain in the terms appropriate to science, but there does not seem to me any objection on scientific grounds to making this a working assumption and then black-boxing it. That said, it is clear that if the cosmos did originate as a point of immense (but finite) energy, its point source can only exist in a higher dimensioned reality, for the simple reason that normal three-dimensional space did not exist at that instant. Thus any science which feels compelled to seek the origin of normal space time will need to break radically with previous assumptions and, in effect, start again on new metascientific foundations. Such disjunctions are, of course, Kuhn's famous paradigm shifts, and they are resisted by what he called "normal science."

Dawkins fights under the evolutionary banner, and seems to assume that neo-Darwinism has answered all the important questions about evolution. His treatment of Intelligent Design is dismissive, as one would expect, but so great is his need to keep the myth of the "blind watchmaker" intact that he has to exclude any evidence to the contrary, and goes out of his way to rubbish those of his fellow zoologists and palaeontologists who wonder about the gaps in the fossil record. Typically, he sweeps away their legitimate questions in the section, "The Worship of Gaps". This is a most worrying sign of the intellectual intolerance of which he accuses all religions and of which sees himself as an indomitable foe. That "chance and necessity" play an essential part in biological processes is not at issue; that they give a full explanation is an act of faith that is becoming increasingly untenable in the face of mounting evidence to those who do not wear the same ideological blinkers as Dawkins.

God and Religion Evolving

Dawkins evolutionary mindset is curiously absent, however, when it comes to religion, for while he shows an impressively wide knowledge of the world's religions, the fact that higher religions and higher spiritual awareness have emerged from the primitive examples he tends to use is never conceded, let alone the possibility or probability of higher forms emerging in the future. This is not reasoned debate but theological street-fighting. Why should we expect Judaism, a late Bronze Age religion (as he notes), to reflect a post-Enlightenment sophistication? The Enlightenment itself did not appear in a cultural vacuum, but has its roots in the fusion of Greek, Jewish, Roman and Christian memes, to use a valuable neologism coined by Dawkins himself. The deepest historical root of the Enlightenment is, without doubt, the Jews' self-conscious worship of "a God of truth". No other culture in the ancient world had remotely such a focus on truth. Even the Greeks, who pursued philosophy, the love of wisdom. had no word *philaletheia*, love of truth, but in the Jewish and Christian mindset it stands out like a rock in a sea of myth and legend. Throughout the Old Testament the God of the Jews is referred to as "the God of truth," and this same spirit continues in the New Testament - "You shall know the truth and the truth will set you free" (John 8:32).

The lack of historical context in making religious judgements must make one uneasy about Dawkins' ultimate conclusions. We are the inheritors of ethical norms that we largely take for granted, but they were once hard won. Western civilisation stands on the shoulders of the Jewish prophets, and a long line of individuals who have suffered for their integrity and courage.

As in science, step-changes are opposed by "orthodoxy," since, by definition, they challenge it with new and unauthorized ways of thinking. One can be sure that when the first prophet told the Jews to stop sacrificing their children in the name of religion, the general reaction, of priests and people, would be a cry of "Heresy!" This general fact is of vital importance, for, if science and religion are continuing to evolve, we can be sure that the next stage of each will be seen as a threat to tradition and will evoke the strongest of passions.

From this perspective, Dawkins' crusade can be seen as a rearguard action, defending an older form of science against an emerging new type. The outlines of the new are unclear, but can be seen in several areas, not least in the appearance of noetics, the science of consciousness, and of ecological science, which is shot through with values, even though mainstream opinion would say that values are anathema to genuine science. The intensity of his argument suggests that he feels his identity as a scientist is being threatened, for it is inseparable from a neo-Darwinian biology which is crumbling at the edges, even though he refuses to acknowledge it. The emotional charge which is felt increasingly throughout Dawkins' work, from *The Selfish Gene* onward makes one suspect that it originates at this subconscious level where one's world-taken-for-granted is being silently undermined. *The God Delusion* is a *tour de force*, but underneath it one may detect a *cri de coeur*.

The Dawkins phenomenon may thus be seen as a response from those share his uncertainties, fears and hopes. It does not only resonate with intellectuals, for it is superb entertainment, and he writes about a subject that "oft was thought but ne'er so well expressed." To say, as he does in *The Independent* interview cited earlier, that "parents forcing their children to accept their religion is a form of child abuse" may be over the top, but it speaks to those who have been subjected in their youth to a kind of oppressive and irrational Christianity that they now wish to escape. Dawkins offers escape through a religion of science, which is, on the surface, rational and noble and intellectually liberating, but is he offering to exchange one form of mental imprisonment for another?

Science as Salvation

In the same interview he complains that "science has an image problem with young people" but, like the bishops faced with empty churches, he seems to be unaware that the problem may be much more than image. The image problem of science has several very real causes, three of which are worth brief mention to indicate how the ideals of science have been sullied as much as those of Christianity. It should perhaps be noted here that Dawkins says Christianity is his prime target: "For most of my purposes, all three Abrahamic religions can be treated as indistinguishable. Unless otherwise stated, I shall have Christianity mostly in mind [and] I shall not be concerned at all with other religions such as Buddhism or Confucianism" (p. 58). The aim of Buddhism is to avoid suffering by becoming enlightened, and that involves ridding oneself of delusions and emotional attachments, among which is the relevance of a higher power to human existence. There is a vast unanswered question beneath Dawkins' kid glove treatment of Buddhism: authentic religion should without doubt be about enlightenment, but should it be ultimately about the avoidance of suffering? It is significant that Christopher Hitchens, the other popular scourge of religion, specifically includes Buddhism as a subject for attack in his best-selling *God is Not Great* (2007).

Dawkins' gospel of science is undermined far more than he recognizes by the way in which its theoretical ideas have been compromised, just as in religion, and in three major respects. Firstly, the alliance of research and technology with the political, military and industrial complex has created an ideological monster which goes under the name of "Big Science". Secondly, in universities and research institutes the demands of publish or perish and the stranglehold of grant committees have buried the ideal of science as the open and cooperative pursuit of truth for its own sake. As the theoretical physicist Michael Duff has put it, "Competition in academia is cut-throat and the British notion of 'fair play' does not apply."[7] Thirdly, in many branches of science, the mathematical (or, more accurately, the algebraic) model has become so hypertrophied that it is now not only "the secret of the temple," as far as the average non-scientist is concerned, but even divides scientific disciplines into non-communicating mathematical specialisms. This state of affairs is particularly scandalous in physics and economics. Science is already a sort of secular religion, with its own priestly authority and articles of belief, speaking often with the same infallible assurance that Dawkins brings to bear on matters that are anything but certain. It is largely immune from questioning, because the ordinary, even the well-educated, person who is not a professional scientist does not have the necessary expertise in mathematics to question or even to understand. Despite the best efforts of scientific popularisers, non-scientists are like the faithful flock in the pews who must trust those with authority.

Dawkins answers to the need of those who seek a reassurance no longer available from the churches and the Bible, but who are unaware that the authority of science is suspect. The steady flow of books with titles such as *The End of Science, The End of Certainty, The End of Physics, The Trouble with Physics. Kicking the Sacred Cow,* etc., is evidence that some revolutionary change is in the offing. He also answers to those who value the independence of mind and freedom of spirit which they have enjoyed since religion declined in the West, but perhaps hope that going along with the scientists will restore a sense of community without infringing on their new found intellectual freedom. Dawkins takes their doubts seriously, which the churches do not. He appeals to those who reject a morality handed down from an imaginary God and who wish to take adult responsibility for their actions, but he also appeals to those who want no God in their lives to provide moral restraint, and this factor is easily overlooked. The breakdown of religious culture has enabled all manner of unethical practices to stake a claim on our conscience. So there is a wide spectrum of attitudes to which Dawkins appeals, from the idealist to the exact opposite.

God Proved Experientially

It might be objected that Dawkins' logical arguments are irrelevant, since the existence of God is proved by the experience that many people have of some otherworldly reality. To quote from Thomas Kelly's *The Reality of the Spiritual World,* "There is a wholly different way of being sure that God is real. It is not an intellectual proof [but] the fact that men experience the presence of God .... In such times of direct experience of Presence, we know that God is utterly real. We need no arguments. When we are gazing into the sun we need no argument, no proof that the sun is shining."[8] The experience has been well attested throughout the ages, in terms similar to those used by a recent writer in *The Times,* who says she had "rejected the possibility of God altogether," but later tells of an occasion when "the world seemed to dissolve around me. It was like dropping through a trap door into darkness, and I found myself in what I can describe only as a sea of sparkling energy. Although I was conscious, nothing, including my body, had any form or structure. At first I was astonished, then I realized that ... this was what people call God, for the sake of calling it something." [9]

Dawkins is too seasoned a campaigner to be taken in by this, and in a section entitled "The Argument from Personal Experience" he simply equates this sense of presence with subjective delusions of the grosser kind, recounting the story of a friend who was convinced that he had heard the devil shrieking, but had probably been fooled in the darkness of the night by the cry of the Manx shearwater. Then, he piles on more ridicule by talking about the conviction of paranoid schizophrenics who are convinced that they are Christ or Napoleon, all to support his case that transcendental experience is an illusion in every instance. This is simply not good enough, for history provides us with innumerable examples of people with the greatest intelligence and integrity reporting of the experience of God. If he had taken the trouble to go a little deeper into the literature, and reported honestly, he would have had to include these positive examples. It is surely significant that the bibliography of *The God Delusion* does not include William James' classical work, *The Varieties of Religious Experience*, which has the objectivity so manifestly missing in this crucial part of his demolition job.

More importantly, a deeper and less cynical understanding of the literature of spiritual experience would have shown him the touchstone of authenticity, namely the change for the better in human nature that follows from the experience of God. It is a *sine qua non* of authentic religion that divine raptures are meaningless if they do not issue in solid virtues. Kelly is completely typical in emphasizing this point. A genuine encounter with God, he says, "strengthens and invigorates our whole personality and *makes us new creatures* .... The tempests and inner strains of self-seeking, self-oriented living grow still." [*op cit.* p. 34, my emphasis]. This is a developmental principle of the utmost importance to psychological theory, and indeed to the future of the species,

Once this simple logic is understood, it can be seen that arguing for or against Dawkins' atheism is shadow-boxing. The real issues are not belief or non-belief in the existence of a divine reality, but whether or not one seeks a relationship with it and what kind of relationship. Authentic religion, as against the parodies that Dawkins often invokes, issues in a transforming relationship and deepening identification with the power which is hypothesized as the source of physical reality, and thus the source of our existence. There is grow-ing awareness that a religion whose purpose is to worship a divine potentate in a heavenly realm is dysfunctional, but less awareness that a paradigm shift is now taking shape in which religion is defined in experiential and transformative terms. What Dawkins misses entirely is the possibility of a new kind of religion crystallizing round a kind of spiritual awareness which previously would have been considered for the exceptional few. On the other hand, he might consider an habitual sense of the divine reality as the worst kind of delusion.

Conclusion

Whatever criticism may be made of his arguments, Dawkins deserves to be taken seriously, for three quite different reasons. Firstly, like Bishop John Robinson's *Honest to God* some forty years ago, *The God Delusion* speaks to a post-Christian society, but now one genera-tion further away from the ages of faith. In his lapidary poem *Dover Beach* Thomas Arnold wrote of "the long withdrawing roar" of the tide of Christianity. That was in 1867, and by now the tide is so far out as to be hardly audible. Against Robinson, Dawkins is saying that traditional Christianity, is no longer even a partial solution but part of the problem, for it no longer answers the questions which beset modern man: Who am I? What is the purpose of life? What is the meaning of existence?

Secondly, he speaks for many sincere individuals who share his epistemological blind spot, the assumption that reality ends at the limits of human sense experience and the present state of human logic. Science has become trapped in this quite unscientific mindset, which might be called the ontological catastrophe, the largely uncon-scious assumption that reality is three-dimensional. This has come about because of Descartes' diktat that science's remit is limited to providing sure and quantifiable knowledge about three dimensional objects. However, as earlier noted, cosmology is now leading us to a post-Cartesian world-view, in which our universe is understood as a subspace of a higher-dimensioned reality. That we cannot visualize it does not make it less real. In offering a new creation story, science has something of vital importance to say to religion, but neither clas-sical religion nor quantum science are able to incorporate the new knowledge. Dawkins's dogmatic blindness is of a piece with that of the equally aggressive atheist Polly Toynbee, recently elected presi-dent of the British Humanist Association, who can state fearlessly that "the here and now is all there is." What, one may ask, makes her so sure?

Thirdly, and perhaps most importantly, Dawkins speaks for those who live habitually in a world where healthy individualism is too often confused with the pathology of selfishness. The Christian world now passing away (in the West at least) put God at the centre of everything, but a kind of reverse Copernicanism has now taken hold, a world view in which "my rights," "my opinion," "my happiness" – even "my spirituality" – have become the centre, the sense of community decays and society becomes dysfunctional. While we cannot return to the sort of Christian world view that Dawkins hammers so relentlessly, it must be said that a world in which a higher reality and purpose is assumed, has a different psychological centre from the a-theistic world that Dawkins inhabits and promotes. Passive, socially conditioned belief in the existence of a creating power may be quite rational but it is sterile, whereas an active, probing belief in the same power, and a bit of humility, is dynamic. It issues over time in deepening awareness that *I am because God is*. This may begin in simple wonderment, but its unfolding reveals human consciousness of a different kind, well attested in literature going back as far as the Hindu Vedas.

At the same time, psychology and anthropology assure us that *God is because I am*, and this is the truth that Dawkins develops with so much skill and energy. Can both premises be correct?

In the past, the answer would have to be "No," but science has revealed two critical new factors, which theology on its own could never have discovered. Knowledge that our universe emerged in time, gives empirical support to a creation event and the basis for rational belief in the existence of a creating power of some kind. By the same token, brain science and social psychology leave us in no doubt that we create the god that answers to our psychological needs. The great weakness of Dawkins' position is that he has no sense of the potential for human development that comes from keeping these two great truths – the creating and created God - in dynamic balance. By concentrating all his attention on the latter, he offers a solution of illusory simplicity. He speaks to, and for, those who know that superstition has had its day, and for that we may be grateful, but he leaves the genuine seeker of scientific and spiritual truth unsatisfied.

References

1. Richard Dawkins, *The God Delusion*. London: Bantam, 2006). What he considers his most important work, *The Extended Phenotype*, receives only passing mention (on page 192), though the gene/phenotype relationship offers the most interesting parallels with the spirituality/religion opposition which many today regard as critically important. For reasons of space I have detoured round this fascinating topic.

2. Adam Hochschild, *Bury the chains: The British Struggle to Abolish Slavery*. Pan Books, 2005, p. 97.

3. Oliver Thomson, *A History of Sin* (Edinburgh: Canongate Press, 1993. p. 259).

4. In a "You Ask The Question Special". *The Independent*. Dec. 4, 2006.

5. Unless we exclude renormalisation, dividing the equations through by infinities to cancel out the ones we wish to go away. Richard Feynman, who invented the technique, called it "dippy". Dirac considered it the fatal fudge in quantum physics.

6. In the *Independent* article cited in note 5.

7. In Peter Woit, *Not Even Wrong: The Failure of String Theory and the Continuing Challenge to Unify the Laws of Physics*. London: Vintage Books, 2007. p. 238.

8. Thomas Kelly, *The Reality of the Spiritual World*. (1944). London: Quaker Home Service, 1996. p. 16.

9. Catherine Lucas, on a page headed "Emotional Intelligence" in *The Times*, 24.12.03

CLASSICAL CHRISTIANITY
AS AN OBSTACLE TO TRUTH*

Christianity has gone through several phases since it first appeared as an insignificant sect of Judaism. The most important of these was the official break with Judaism, the religion of its founder, which happened in the year 83, when followers of Jesus were ejected from the synagogue and ritually cursed. Although there have been many dramatic changes in Christianity since then, resulting in a multiplicity of churches, there has been common agreement about two things, namely the historical accuracy of the New Testament and the articles of the Nicene Creed. The Creed is essentially a summary statement of the assumed historical facts, and in effect a common constitution. Agreement on these matters of faith has endured until the present and justifies treating Christianity, despite its many internal differences, as a single entity and using the term "classical" as an umbrella term for post-Nicene Christianity.

Classical Christianity is in steep decline in the West, not just shrinking in numbers and cultural influence but now widely seen by many well meaning people as regressive and superstitious. Given that it provided the intellectual foundation and the inspiration for Western civilization, it is natural, indeed urgent, to ask why it has lost its ability to inspire, and I will argue that, among many reasons, the main and critical one is theological. In particular, the spiritual dynamic of Christianity has been sapped by the gap that has appeared between historical fact and Christian mythology. Whether wilful or not, a dishonesty has grown at the heart of Christianity as science and historical scholarship have thrown its central narrative into question.

In this regard, the Jewish historian Norman Cantor has words about his own religion which are equally applicable to Christianity. Noting that "Orthodox Jews in their early morning prayers daily thank God for making the Jews 'different than the peoples of the earth,'" he sees Judaism's loss of spiritual dynamic and its claim to spiritual leadership in its unwillingness or inability to come to terms with the modern world. The Jews have, as he puts it, "bowed out of historicity while they were ahead."[1] In another place, he makes the point more forcefully, "It is time we told the truth about Jewish history [which is] nothing more than a ... myth, a work of imaginative fiction."[2]

---

*Amended version of an article first published in *Faith and Freedom: A Journal of Progressive Religion*. Vol 55, part 1, 2002.

Like Judaism, Christianity is in thrall to its own mythology, and it is interesting that while Christian believers hold to the literal truth of the miracles of Jesus, which are taken as proof that he was the only son of God, similar wonders in the Old Testament are not given the same significance, and indeed are not necessarily regarded as believable. Thus while it is critically important that Jesus multiplied loaves, brings the dead Lazarus to life and ascends bodily to heaven, the same actions performed by Elisha, who also multiplies loaves, brings a dead child to life (2 Kings 4 & 5) and goes up to heaven on a whirlwind (2 Kings 2:11) are merely parts of the rich pattern of wonders which is woven into the Old Testament. In both instances, theses stories served a valuable purpose in a time when the difference between historical fact and fable were not regarded as important, but we live in times where truth is differently, and more rigorously, defined, and we cannot turn the clock back and make ourselves think like illiterate people in a pre-scientific age, merely to keep intact the form of an earlier version of Christianity. Yet this is, in fact, what the Christian churches demand of their members.

For many it will come as a surprise that Christianity has gone through different phases, and that what now is regarded as "orthodoxy" did not take on its form until three centuries after the death of Jesus. The very first Christians were Jews, and the head of the Jesus movement was his younger brother James with whom Paul negotiated for the freedom to enrol non-Jews into the movement. As he records in Galatians (2:9), they shook hands on the deal in a public statement of fellowship between Jews and gentiles in the Jesus movement.[3] But there were theological reefs ahead that were to bring this sincere attempt at union to grief. For the first Christians Jesus was the awaited Messiah, the son of David and the greatest of the prophets "in whom the scriptures were fulfilled". The rapidly increasing gentile converts, however, who did not share the Jewish world view and were ignorant of its history, struggled to find a theory of Jesus to account for their unquenchable feeling that he was not only the greatest of the Jews but a uniquely significant human being - a man for the Roman empire and for the world, a man for the present and the future.

With the conversion of Constantine to Christianity the debate was resolved in an unexpected way, for he substituted Jesus for the supreme Roman divinity *Sol Invictus*, the Sun God, and many aspects of both religions became merged. Since the "birth" of the sun was celebrated in December at the time of the winter solstice, it was not unnatural to celebrate the birthday of Jesus as a replacement. The transition was not so abrupt as it might seem, for shortly after this we find Christians giving Jesus the very appropriate title *Sol Justitiae*, sun of righteousness. It was natural also to combine celebrations of the birth of Christ with the feast of Saturnalia, which was a sort of mid-winter carnival to brighten up the dark days ahead until spring reappeared. Saturnalia under various guises was widespread in Europe, and doubtless elsewhere, having originated as an agricultural feast. This is not really surprising, since religion in an agricultural age was a worship of nature through its seasonal "births" and "deaths", its sowings and harvestings. Until recently in England, for instance, the return of spring was celebrated by dancing round the maypole, whose religious origins as a phallic fertility symbol have now been largely lost to view. A good crop was a matter of life and death in earlier times, and hence propitiation of the gods of fertility was of central religious importance, so much so that in Attic Greece, the midwinter festival was celebrated with human sacrifice. To celebrate the birth of a God-man with mythical offerings of gold, frankincense and myrrh is certainly an improvement on that! Christmas Day was also a good opportunity for Christianity to absorb Mithraism, its great rival in the late Roman Empire, for the religion of Mithras, which had as it central motif the killing of a mythical bull (a symbol of crude animistic religion) by a kind of astrological saviour-figure. This was celebrated in Mithraism as the dawning of the new Age of Pisces, very much as New Agers today celebrate the emerging Age of Aquarius. Thus by the most direct inference the death and resurrection of Jesus was preached as the signal of a new age of salvation for the world. It all made marvellous sense in those days.

These changes were able to happen smoothly because the ancient sacrificial religions found an echo in Paul's doctrine of the sacrifice of Jesus on the cross. Of course, Jesus was not sacrificed, but executed as a political threat by the Roman governor, abetted and probably incited by the puppet government of the Jewish priesthood. Nevertheless, Paul's myth of sacrificial atonement struck an answering chord in the minds of people for whom religion centred on sacrifice, and it lives on, and is, indeed, for many Christians the essence of Christianity itself. For non-Christians and ex-Christians, however, a divinely sacrificial Christ is no longer a myth in the dynamic and life-giving sense, but in the purely negative sense of a non-truth, a fiction. It does not illuminate, it obscures.

In relating the Christian year to the calendar of the fertility religions and in making the purpose of Jesus's existence on earth a sacrifice of atonement, the early Church may have helped the people of that time to accept the new religion, but the price paid was to diminish awareness that Christianity was a new kind of religion. Its unique power to inspire lay not in worshipping a different God but in its call to emulate the man Jesus in whom divinity was felt to reside. By presenting Jesus as a sacrificial "lamb of God" within the framework of a noble fertility myth of birth, death and resurrection, Christianity was able to speak to a bygone age in language that they could understand, but it ran the risk of losing the essential Christian message, which is, to use the title of Thomas a Kempis's famous devotional work, *The Imitation of Christ*. Nevertheless, we can see from our vantage point in history that without the myth so dramatically re-enacted in the liturgy of Christmas, Good Friday and Easter, it is doubtful that a living Christianity in any form would have survived. The Jewish Ebionite community, which held to a "pure" and primitive form of the teaching handed on by Jesus drifted out of history within a century of his death.

To people in the 20th century, however, what might be called the canonical myth presents so great an intellectual and emotional obstacle that even churchmen disagree on the fundamentals. (See endnote 4 for references in this paragraph.) Bishop Jenkins caused outrage by questioning the bodily resurrection of Jesus and dismissing the literal resurrection stories in the gospel as hardly more than "a conjuring trick with bones." John Macquarrie, less provocative, probably speaks for the great majority of scriptural scholars today - and for those ministers who learned their Christology within the past thirty years - when he says that "the birth narratives ... are manifestly legendary in character". The late Raymond Brown, perhaps the most authoritative Catholic commentator, and a recognized conservative, is forced to admit that "the biblical evidence leaves the question of the historicity of the virginal conception unresolved." John Polkinghorne, eminent scientist and ordained minister believes, on the other hand, accepts the virginal conception as a credible option but dismisses the Ascension as "quaint" and altogether too naive for the modern mind. (In passing, it may be noted that if a bodily ascension is ruled out, the Christian must find some other way of ending the story of a resurrected Jesus.) The late Canon Arthur Peacocke, winner of the prestigious Templeton Prize for progress in science and theology, has no difficulty in declaring that science puts paid to both the Virgin Birth (to use the popular term) and the Ascension but cannot be called upon in the search for truth in the case of the Resurrection, because the New Testament story "can properly be claimed to be referring to a new kind of reality, hitherto unknown ... on which the sciences as such can make no comment." If the seeker after truth today is to be true to his or her conscience, they must ask what specifically is it about this "new kind of reality" that puts the Resurrection beyond the bounds of normal scientific enquiry.

A complete answer to this question must inevitably be lengthy, for it will need to take in matters of historical context, cultural and philosophical assumptions and psychology. First, it needs to be understood that this kind of out-of-bounds question is to be found not only in all existing religions but in science too. No Moslem may question that the Koran is the final revelation of God, no physicist may question the laws of thermodynamics with impunity, no biologist may question the belief that evidence of purpose in evolution is illusory. It would be both naïve and dishonest to single out Christians for going into denial when fundamental beliefs are put under scrutiny, for one's sense of identity is often inseparable from such beliefs. Biblical scholarship has steadily stripped away the lesser or more illogical myths, like the outer layers of an onion, but the process never seems to go down as far as open questioning of the factuality of the bodily resurrection of Jesus. This has, of course, been questioned and rejected by some academic theologians (perhaps Rudolf Bultman most famously) but not by public churchmen, the reason for this, one may presume, being fear that if the literal resurrection were to go, Christianity itself would disappear with it, like the onion whose last layer had been peeled away.

Bishops Jenkins and Spong are almost alone in seeing and publicly preaching the resurrection story without prevarication as symbolic of some other reality, a happening or, more likely, a series of happenings of an essentially psychological kind of such power that they inspired the first Christians to come together as a missionary group to spread the teaching of Jesus. There is every reason to think that the Pentecost story is the other half of an account of a group experience which assured the first Christians that the spirit of Jesus lived on, but since that is not the way the story is told in the New Testament, this does not at first appear a strong position, and the literal historical truth of the Resurrection seems to stand on its own. The plausibility of the symbolic and non-literalist interpretation increases, however, when it is considered that the gospels were written between twenty and fifty years after Paul preached the bodily resurrection in his letters to young churches. There is, therefore, circumstantial evidence at least that Paul's interpretation of Christianity - "my gospel", as he calls it in Romans 2:16 - had a great influence on the four canonical gospels and that his personal Resurrection story became part of what later was written as history.

Belief in the literal resurrection of Jesus continues to be a linchpin of Christian doctrine, despite all the many anomalies surrounding it, partly because St Paul insisted to the early church that "If Christ was not raised, our faith is null and void" (1 Cor 15:13), partly because this belief has become so embedded in the doctrinal elaborations of Christianity, its creeds and liturgies, that it would seem impossible to replace it without demolishing Christianity altogether. It is perhaps worthwhile to note that Paul faced up to a similar accusation of demolishing Judaism, and thus Judaic Christianity,[5] when he preached his version of the Jesus narrative, which he was not ashamed to say was idiosyncratic. Indeed, he boasted, "No man taught it to me; I received it through a revelation of Jesus Christ" (Gal. 1:12). We may gain some insight into his motives for preaching the physically resurrected Jesus in considering that for him Jesus was the new Adam, and Adam was the human being who had brought death into the world, so there was an obvious symmetry in presenting Jesus as one who had overcome death. Further, Paul believed with the first generation of Christians (and still some today) that Jesus would come again to earth "on the clouds of heaven" to inaugurate the reign of God. Hence the continuing physical existence of a Jesus, who conquered death, became almost a logical necessity.

When pressed, Paul falls back on what can only be described, if we are to be honest, as bluster and logical sleight of hand. "You may ask, how are the dead raised? In what kind of body? A senseless question! .... All flesh is not the same flesh: there is flesh of men, flesh of beasts of birds, and of fishes - all different. There are heavenly bodies and earthly bodies .... So it is with the resurrection of the dead .... sown as an animal body, it is raised as a spiritual body" (1 Cor 15:35 ff). His readers presumably were not so troubled by the contradiction as we are today, but we do not know if any asked Paul later what kind of thing a spiritual body might be - was it a body or not? It is at least clear from the mode of argumentation that the body of the resurrected Christ was of this ambiguously spiritual kind. Some three of four years after the supposed ascension into heaven the resurrected Jesus appeared to Paul, as recounted in 1 Cor. 15:5 and in Luke's *Acts of the Apostles*. Neither Paul nor Luke, however gives reason to think that this life-changing event in his life involved a corporeal presence. Many throughout history have reported and continue to report inspirational appearances of Jesus. The question of a flesh and blood Christ is hardly relevant in such situations: the experience is too real to deny, and nothing would be gained by inventing a corporeal, rather than spiritual, presence. The existence of a transforming Christianity depends not upon the living on of a once dead body but of a new kind of human consciousness.

Why, then, do honest and scholarly people feel the need to insist that Christianity stands or falls by belief in the bodily resurrection of Jesus? For those with positions in the Church there is the obvious reason that a livelihood will be lost and if there is a family to support there will be a real split of conscience. For the rank and file Christian there is no leadership within the churches to help those with doubts and nowhere obviously better to go if they were to leave. Overall, there is within the Christian body an inertia compounded of loyalty to an institution which continues to do much good and offer spiritual comfort and traditional values which are wired deep in our mind. The end result is a half-conscious fear that in abandoning the pivotal Christian myth, one's sense of identity would be weakened. And so the whole mythical system remains intact, as what used to be called "the ark of salvation" drifts away from the shore of the modern world.

The Christian myth once had a powerful unifying effect, over-riding other religious cultures and bringing into the unity of Christendom Roman and Greek, Celt, German and Slav, but now it divides, even within the Church itself. Where belief in the myth is totally unquestionable we see the baneful effects of Christian fundamentalism, which is, in effect, a state of complete group denial. Members of mainstream churches may be said to live in partial denial, but would-be Christians in a scientific age feel their integrity challenged by a religious group which demands that they selectively suspend their normal criteria for truth. For such seekers classical Christianity becomes a desirable ideal but at the same time an impossible belief system. It is inevitable that traditional Christian belief originally framed within a flat earth world view creates for modern man what psychologists call cognitive dissonance.

The popular poet John Betjeman expressed this dilemma in a nostalgic poem about Christmas, in which he talks of the warm feelings generated by country churches, lamplight, carols, the crib, etc. but then suddenly asks:

> *And is it true? And is it true,*
> *This most tremendous tale of all ...*
> *The Maker of the stars and sea*
> *Became a child one earth for me?*

Historically, of course, it is not true, which is what causes Betjeman's unease to surface, as it does from time to time in most thinking Christans. To be honest to himself he must accept that genuine religion today must be true as far as possible to historical and scientific fact. To call anything a religion of truth which is based on legend and fiction, however creative that fiction might be, is to abuse the term.

Such criticism must, however, be handled carefully, for until recently principled honesty to the historical and scientific facts was possible in only a limited way, and thus no religion could regard them as essential. It is only within the last generation that the Genesis story of creation of the world could be superseded with the theory of an expanding universe, and not even the most hardened sceptic could have questioned the Adam and Eve story two centuries ago. The marvel is that the writer of Genesis could have got so many of the essentials so right, as may be appreciated by comparing the biblical account with the bizarre creation myths of other religions.[6]

At the same time, under the symbolism of the Christmas story and salvation history in general there is certainly a most tremendous truth, and many would argue that the way to solve the present crisis in Christianity is to extract the truth from its symbolical and mythological framework, deal with this essential or core truth separately, through scholarly analysis and meditation, but continue to use the mythological framework as before. This seemingly plausible solution is, in fact, illusory, for we can rarely separate the truth so cleanly from the symbols through which it is transmitted and understood. Indeed, language itself is made up of what have been called "dead metaphors". Do we really think, for instance, that we get into hot water when we get into hot water – so to speak. Small wonder, then, that myth, which is metaphor on a larger scale, becomes first pressed into service to communicate theological truth and then becomes identified with it. Science has its myths, hardly less naive than fairy tales, so it does not automatically offer an answer to religion seeking factual truth. We live by myths whose poetical, artistic or dramatic form and their "inner" meaning are seamlessly joined, often quite unconsciously. As Marshall McLuhan famously said, "The medium is the message."

Despite the definitive pronouncement of the Council of Chalcedon in 451 that Jesus was totally human, Christian teaching must gloss over what this means in order to present him as a divine being pre-existing in heaven. Besides, he is conventionally presented as a sinless man, and what kind of human being never sinned or felt remorse? This latent contradiction ultimately forces us to define Christianity in one or other of two incompatible ways. We can either iconize the historical Jesus and worship him as a quasi-divinity or strive to imitate him as a human centred on God, for whom the subordination of what might be called his natural will to divine will was "meat and drink". This is the self-description that John's gospel put in his mouth (4:34), and this is what sets him apart from from ordinary humanity and makes him the embodiment of a spiritual challenge. Not all would find the mindset of Jesus inspirational, and if we are to believe Mark's gospel, even his own family seemed to see it as a kind a madness and tried to put him under restraint (3:20). This is not a passage that is often taken as a text for preaching, but it contains a powerful truth – the deepest spirituality is abnormal and alien to the ordinary human. In any event, if Jesus is regarded as a God, there is obviously not much point in trying to imitate him, our natural relationship to him must be one of adoration. If, on the other hand, he is regarded as a higher form of humanity, he can be seen quite naturally as the realisation of all our human potential. In the latter case religious faith becomes belief that in "taking on the mind of Christ", as Paul expressed it (*Philippians* 2:5) we shall find the way to unlock our unrealised, and previously unimagined, potential and gain a new kind of self-fulfilment. The choice we face today is not so clearcut, however, for, whatever may be the drawbacks of the orthodox myth, it has a powerful psychological hold, even for those who would not consider themselves Christian: its beauty and power are woven into our consciousness and our culture.

To overcome the gravitational pull of our cultural past, a new kind of story for a new kind of religion is needed, at least as a complement to the old, answering to the needs of a mature adult in a scientific age. Whatever is to take humanity into the future can only do so by making a break with the past where a break is needed, while developing the living part of tradition. It cannot be a tinkering or a fudge, for it must be a finer religion than anything now existing. At the same time, it must be simple in outline and robust in structure, for it must survive in the marketplace as well as on the mountain top or in the convent chapel. It must have a clear spiritual focus, as against traditional religion in which tribal or ethnic loyalty is inseparably mixed up with the ethical and spiritual. An authentic religion today must, quite simply, transform us into a new kind of human being, for unless this new human being emerges and spreads across the globe, there is no future for our race and our planet. It must make us happy, but happy in a way we have not yet experienced, or perhaps have experienced only in rare moments of oneness with creation and with our fellow human beings. It must change us into creatures for whom love is an instinct and awareness of God-in-all-things a reflex, and it must reach down to those for whom life is a broken, despairing, often suicidal sort of thing for whom the ancient myths of religion do nothing but add to their despair.

That we owe an enormous debt to classical Christianity can hardly be contested. It brought into existence a whole civilization which, whatever its limitations, has taught the world about the value of the individual, about justice for all, about the necessity of democratic government and the beauty of scientific truth. It is logical, therefore, to look to the future as a development of the Judaeo-Christian tradition, even though the changes now required may seem to deny rather than develop the core truth of Christianity. One of the problems which must now be faced is that the developable elements of Christianity are embedded in the mythology, thus making it difficult to keep the best and reject the rest. What can be said without doubt is that Paul's intuitive understanding that Jesus was "the new man" and "the first born of a great new human family" is an evolutionary statement made nearly two thousand years before the concept of evolution started to dawn in science. To communicate its significance we need now to call upon the different sciences – biological, palaeological, psycho-logical, and others – which will lead to new insight about the nature of spirituality and its corporate form, religion. In turn these insights must issue in new kinds of structures and practices appropriate to a rapidly globalizing humanity, but in order to make progress into this imagined future we must first identify the deepest truth of Christian-ity and leave behind its classical, mythological formulation. Without doubt, it will be the longest and most painful of goodbyes.

References

1. Norman Cantor, *The Sacred Chain: A History of the Jews.* London: Fontana, 1996. pp. 17,16.

2. "Is this the final chapter in the Jews' glorious history," *Sunday Times*, Aug. 20, 1995.

3. The path of divergence can be traced from this point. Paul's en-thusiastic agreement to "keep the poor of Jerusalem in mind" is a euphemism for what was in effect payment for a franchise. The nub of the agreement was that he could continue to preach his highly suspect version of Christianity to gentiles but well away from the centre of operations. It is clear that this payment became increasingly inadequate to balance the inroads that his gospel was making into the Judaic Jesus movement, and Paul reveals in *Romans* 15 his fear that the Jerusalem church would withdraw his licence to preach it. The split between a Hellenic and Judaic Jesus had become too great to be bridged by any compromise or monetary payment.

4. Citations in order from:

   John Macquarrie, *Jesus Christ in Modern Thought.* London: SCM, 1990. p. 392.

   Raymond E. Brown, *The Birth of the Messiah.* London: Chapman, 1977. p. 527.

John Polkinghorne, *Science and Christian Belief*. London: SPCK, 1997 [1994]. p. 121.

Arthur Peacocke, *God and Science: A Quest for Christian Credibility*. London: SCM. 1996. p. 77.

5. The accusation, as recounted in *Acts*, 21, was that Paul "spreads *his* doctrines [emphasis added] all over the world attacking our people, our law, and this sanctuary [sc. the temple in Jerusalem]". In the crowd who yelled, "Kill him!" (21:36), it is more than possible that there were Jewish Christians.

6. *Genesis* also contains fragments of another (perhaps Babylonian) myth of human creation happening through the sons of God marrying the women of this earth (Genesis 6:2). The Koran contains the Genesis myth of man's emergence from clay, by way of an unspecified "germ" and a clot of blood (23:1) but also remnants of the ancient Egyptian myth that the universe was created from the semen of a divine male being (53:33).

Part 2:
LOOKING FORWARD:
NEOSCIENCE

This section is in some ways the heart of the book, in that it proposes a theory of reality as a new basis for both for science and religious belief.

The first essay shows how Hubble's discovery of the galactic redshift calls for a recentring of the universe, in the same way that Copernicus's theory once recentred the universe on the sun, rather than the earth.

The second argues with specific examples that Einsteinian relativity is now blocking progress to understanding both the quantum and the cosmos.

The third essay is a sketch of Darwin's world view and the evidence now revealing its limitations and, at the same time, a call for his kind of vision and integrity.

Three revolutions are needed, and will be resisted. To quote from Werner Heisenberg:

> When new groups of phenomena compel changes in the pattern of thought, even the most eminent of physicists find immense difficulties .... Once one has experienced the desperation with which men of science react to the demand for a change in the thought pattern, one can only be amazed that such revolutions in science have actually been possible at all.

> *Across the Frontiers,*
> NY: Harper & Row, 1974, p. 162

BEFORE THE BIG BANG

Well, of course, there was no "before" before the Big Bang, since time itself came into existence at that point, and the notion that time had a beginning leaves natural science with a huge problem of identity, since whatever a timeless reality might turn out to be, it certainly is not nature as science has always known it. Hubble's discovery of the galactic redshift has put us on a slippery slope that leads to an unnatural science for which we have as yet no name, but **neoscience** will do very well, at least to label the problem at this exploratory stage.

Science's problem, however, is philosophy's great opportunity, perhaps the greatest challenge since Plato, and if there are any philosophical Alexanders out there weeping for new worlds to conquer, they can dry their tears now. It is by no means a totally new challenge, for anyone who embarks upon it will find Zeno's ancient paradox popping up continually, how to bridge the conceptual and mathematical gap between a continuum divided infinitely into smaller bits and zero. Max Planck and his counter-intuitive quantum of energy will offer a helping hand, but let us first get a clearer idea of how to define the problem.

Physicists in general have done us no service here, having blurred its outlines for their own immediate purposes. Winding back in imagination our expanding cosmos to find its origin, they have reached a point where all the laws of physics break down, the so-called "Planck wall", and then stopped the conceptual film. With the notable exception of Alexander Friedmann, the reluctance of physicists to go all the way is understandable, for to go right to the beginning of the film would apparently result in compressing all the energy within the universe to a mathematical point, leaving physical theorists with two great headaches. Not only would they be left with a dimensionless point in a totally timeless realm, but the point would "contain" (if that is the right word) an infinite amount of energy. Understandably, it is very tempting to say that anything beyond the Planck size is too small to matter, twenty orders of magnitude smaller than the proton at the heart of the atom or, to get some sort of visual grasp, a trillion trillion times smaller than a speck of flour. That, surely, is as near as dammit to nothing, but still gives physics something measurable to work on, even though its usual mathematical tools – the wave function, differential equation and system Hamiltonian – all become very rubbery at this dimension.

But then arise two equally thorny questions: how did this minuscule particle of energy get there in the first place, and what started it expanding into the cosmos that we, as scientists, survey from the inside? The first question can be answered, rather arbitrarily, by assuming it had been there for ever (assuming we know what "for ever" means), and the second by invoking, like a *deus ex machina* (the pun is appropriate) a random fluctuation as the start of it all. Since we know so little about what could have happened at the Planck stage, it seems permissible to say that anything could have happened. "Quantum fluctuation" is a decidedly *ad hoc* solution, but it appeals to the modern mind, which likes to put randomness in the unexplained gaps, where once God might have been pressed into service, and its sounds suitably arcane. However, the greatest objection to using random fluctuation at the Planck level as an all-purpose explanation is exactly the same that philosophers level at those who wish to bring in God to explain the gaps: it is a causeless cause.

Two new postulates will give a critically different perspective on the problem. Firstly, if the cosmos is expanding and cooling, as no scientist would deny today, why not treat it as an adiabatic system familiar to heat engineers, as, for instance, in internal combustion and steam engines. And, secondly, if the beginning of the expansionary process was a true point, why not locate it in something other than a three dimensional domain, in the hyperspace beloved of science fiction writers and well known to mathematicians of a certain ilk, but not to be confused with Hilbert space, which is a descriptive convenience with no ontological claims. From this perspective, the normal universe of sense experience must be viewed as a subspace of a higher dimensioned space, perhaps a privileged subspace, but nevertheless only a province of a greater unseen realm.

That there exists a higher dimensioned reality inaccessible to our senses, a domain as real as our three-dimensioned cosmos is, an act of faith, but no more so than believing that reality consists of only of the three dimensions assumed unquestioningly by Cartesian science and commonsense alike. After all, we know that the apparently empty space around us is filled with radio waves which remain silent and unobserved until we tune into them at the right frequency. Is science trapped in an illusion that *res extensa*, being all that natural science can handle, is therefore all that can exist, or is a new kind of science now required to go beyond the present barriers to knowledge? Is science imprisoned in a Cartesian goldfish bowl?

The benefit of approaching cosmology as the study of a system of expanding 3D space and decreasing temperature is that it is conceptually simple and in accordance with the physical facts, so far as we know them, but also that it throws up a question that is strangely unnoticed in mainstream physics and cosmology, namely: what is 3D space expanding into? It is probably fair to say that insofar as this critical question has been addressed, the answers are hardly more than geometrical hand-waving, with vague reference to finite, unbounded surfaces, as exemplified in spherical solids. More on this vital question below.

As regards the energy content of the universe's initial state, unless we take Einstein's General Relativity to be unquestionable, there is absolutely no reason to think that the "naked singularity" must contain an infinity of energy. The amount of energy that it does contain can be calculated from the so-called Planck Density, where gravitational-type energy reaches its extreme limit at 5.1×10^{96} kilograms per cubic centimeter or, somewhat trickier, its equivalent in radiation density. It is a lot, but still finite. We might get some small idea of the magnitude by imagining the weight of Mount Everest sitting on the top of pin. Such a pressure would merit the overused term "awesome".

Now comes the logical key that astronomers and quantum physicists have overlooked, the first law of thermodynamics, which states quite simply that energy can neither be created nor destroyed. Following this logic, rather than the delusory mathematical process of dividing by zero, if the universe is a closed system, its originating point would have contained exactly the same amount of energy as it does at any stage of its expansion. Approaching the cosmos as a thermodynamic system, expanding volume is seen immediately to be inversely proportional to heat density. My chemistry book at school contained this information in the following limerick:

> *These facts you will learn at your school*
> *About Messrs Thomson and Joule,*
> *Who allowed compressed gas*
> *Through a small hole to pass*
> *And expand, then the gas became cool.*

So far, so simple, but how are we to account for the gap between the cosmic "Ur-point" in hyperspace and the first appearance of our 3D cosmos at Planck time? The answer to that is equally simple but, like Planck's principle (initially a wild conjecture) it is counter-intuitive. In fact, it has been blowing logical minds since Zeno. To go from the something of the Planck domain to the nothing of an initial point of immense energy requires only that we push Planck's logic to its limit.

Planck's philosophizing on the nature of radiation led him to the desperate solution that energy comes in an indivisible packet, which he named the quantum, thus launching science into the era of quantum physics. Planck himself hated this idea, for there seemed to be no reason why energy should not be divided again and again *ad infinitum*. He half-suspected that his enforced solution was no more than mathematical trickery, and spent years trying to disprove it, but received the Nobel Prize for it in 1918, by which time, despite its irrationality, it was mainstream science. It is *par excellence* one of those things in science of which Richard Feynman said we get an illusory feeling of understanding which is really no more than the effect of familiarity.

There is no reason *a priori* why Planck's "illogical logic" cannot be applied to closing the cosmological gap, that is to say jumping from a very, very small three-dimensioned actual cosmos to a dimensionless cosmos, which would be a potential waiting to be actualized. Assuming that the Planck domain is as small a size as an energetic particle can be, why not simply say that the next step down is a reality of no dimensions at all, even though we are nagged by the question, why can't we divide it one more time? The answer has to be simply, that's the way reality is. One suffers with Planck, or chuckles with Zeno!

Once this step from something to nothing is accepted, however reluctantly, both science and philosophy confront another problem, equally difficult and probably even more controversial: how did it begin, what triggered it all? If the erudite pseudo-explanation of "quantum fluctuation" is disallowed, why not take a commonsense approach by asking what triggers anything. What, for instance, sets in train the process that ends in the bullet leaving the gun or the rocket setting off for Mars? Viewed as mechanical systems, one can say that the initiating energy which sends the bullet or rocket on its way is the pressure of the finger on the trigger or the button, but before that what energetic cause triggers the action of the finger in such situations? The answer is the conscious intent of the human being who makes the decision. Without an act of intelligent will to start it off, nothing happens.

Such considerations lead to the surmise that our particular universe came into existence as an act of will? Despite orthodox shudders, it is perfectly rational, and an answer in the positive would not be a religious solution, even though religionists might throw their hats in the air. What is often overlooked is that religion proper concerns not belief in a higher power, but belief that humankind is, or can be, in communication with this hypothesized power. Many people have had experience which would support this belief, but many feel no sympathy for it, because they have had no such experience, and they may or may not wish to have it. So proof or disproof must remain a very personal and subjective thing, and thus hardly within the domain of science as we know it. The issue of a creating consciousness is thus a sticking point for science, and takes us into metascience, and considerations as to what constitutes proof. Of this vast and disputed area, little can be said here, but I float one proposal worth consideration, that while deductive and inductive proof have taken science to it present state, we may need to consider other forms if science is not to stagnate, notably systemic coherence and what might be called forensic or jury proof, which occupies a hazy middle ground between subjective and objective, and all tied in with the disciplined imagination of the thought experiment or, since it sounds much more scientific, the *Gedankenexperiment* that Einstein used to such good effect.

Returning to the question of what our expanding 3D cosmos is expanding into, once we postulate that time and three-dimensional space came into existence at the moment of the Big Bang, we must eliminate an answer that the cosmos expands like a balloon inflating into a pre-existing 3-space. The obvious answer is that it is expanding into a previously existing but different-dimensioned space, and seemingly a timeless space. As our cosmos expands, it probably takes time with it wherever it goes. Then follows the question, is this hypothesized space higher- or lower-dimensioned? If this is the reality of things, the leading edge, or surface, of the expanding 3D cosmos would be rather like a wave of state change, where 2-space is stepped up to 3-space, or 4-space or hyperspace stepped down. A partial understanding may perhaps be obtained by considering the state change that occurs when a pellet of solid carbon dioxide is dropped into a beaker of near-freezing water, causing an ice crystal to accrete around it almost instantly in a moving front of ice-formation. The introduction of the dry ice pellet may be considered as trigger energy which starts the process in the same way that a conscious decision to, say, raise one's arm can be considered as trigger energy. A beaker of supersaturated brine will sit indefinitely unchanged if undisturbed, but a phase change can be effected by the slightest input of energy, such as dropping into the beaker a grain of sand, which will immediately precipitate salt crystals out. This may be a valid metaphor for a hyperspatial science, in that our familiar 3D reality may exist *in potentia* until actuated, rather as salt exists invisibly in non-crystalline form when dissolved in water. The metaphor may help in clarifying the ontological status of what appears to be a purely mathematical hyperspace in relation to what seems to human senses a "real" 3D subspace. What begins informally as a mental image of our universe dissolved in something greater can be formalized through topology.

Of the interlocking questions that emerge from a theory of hyperspace, the issue of the energy of consciousness will almost certainly be the most contentious, for the Cartesian dualism that dominates science classifies consciousness uncompromisingly as *res cogitans*, and thus by definition outside the remit of natural science. A curious blindness afflicts mainstream science in this regard, for not only do we have the obvious evidence shown above that consciousness supplies the trigger energy for bodily actions, but there is statistically significant and replicable laboratory evidence that human consciousness can affect mechanical systems. The major work on this has been done by the late Robert Jahn, who has used focused intention, of individuals and groups, to skew the output of electromechanical random number generators. His work is well known and can be found on the Web, but since it does not fit into the current Cartesian paradigm, it is largely ignored. Jahn, it might be said to divert charges of "pseudoscience", is no eccentric or head-in-clouds philosopher, but was the Dean Emeritus of the Mechanical and Aerospace Engineering Department at Princeton University.

In searching for the origins of the Big Bang we are probing into a new scientific paradigm, opening up questions that will certainly be unwelcome to what Thomas Kuhn called "normal scientists", who are usually as conservative in their own way as bishops. Let it be assumed that the energy of consciousness is a reality that science needs now take into account, how could one wake a whole profession from its dogmatic slumber? I would like to suggest an *experimentum crucis*. Let it be transmitted on TV to entertain and educate as many people as possible in the most dramatic way, with a bang.

The experiment would be to wire up explosive charges to a large, preferably very large, building with a demolition order on it, and connect them to a trigger device consisting of a microswitch whose activation needs energy only in the order of the falling grain of sand just mentioned. Then sit a group of people down and ask them to concentrate on activating this switch simply by willing it to flip. It could work, couldn't it? If it didn't, there might be red faces, but if it did work, no one could be in any doubt thereafter that consciousness is a directable form of energy. It makes things happen.

BEYOND EINSTEIN*

DEDICATION

Every scientist and every philosopher must say with Newton that they stand on the shoulders of giants, but a special tribute must be paid here to James Clerk Maxwell, a true giant of science and a man of deep religious sensitivity. By unifying magnetism and electricity, he changed the great aim of physics into the search for a unified theory of all of nature's forces. In so doing, he sowed the seed for a future redefinition, not only of physics but of science itself, a physics which took reality to be more than three-dimensional.

Hyperspace for Maxwell was neither fiction nor purely mathematical imagination: it was, as he said, "the seal of Solomon in three dimensions," an escape from sense limitations through Hamilton's quaternions. I hope this paper will play a small part in reviving the scientific interest in hyperspace which Maxwell had hoped to do, by bringing to bear empirical evidence that science is still uncovering but which was unavailable to him.

Introduction

To avoid misunderstanding I should say in advance that I write not as a professional physicist or cosmologist but as a philosopher of evolution with a particular interest in the nature of science in its relation to truth and reality. The distinction between science and philosophy is not always easy to maintain, for, as Einstein asserted, "reality is the real business of physics," and reality is also the real business of both philosophy and theology too – or at least, it should be.

The underlying assumption of this paper, which needs to be made explicit, is that both science and religion evolve through incremental steps punctuated by disjunctions, which Thomas Kuhn called paradigm changes, when new ways of perceiving and modelling physical reality are born. The classic example of a scientific paradigm is, of

*Expanded and revised version of a paper delivered to the Science and Religion Forum Conference on *Einstein, God and Time* at the Clarendon Laboratory, Oxford, 13/9/2005

course, the Copernican revolution, when humankind stopped seeing the earth as the centre of the universe and, reluctantly, started to look out at a universe centred on the sun. This was of fundamental importance not only for astronomy but for human evolution, because it enabled us, firstly, to look at the earth from the outside in imagination and thus released us from the prison of direct sense impression. Secondly, it opened up the possibility that some day science might discover a larger universe with a different centre. This has, of course, happened, as astronomical observation went on to reveal that what we once thought was the total of physical reality is actually a small part of a galaxy, and then that our galaxy is a small part of a cosmos made up of billions of such galaxies. We have redefined the "universe," and the true scientist should now be prepared for the intellectual shock of redefining it again.

The proposal of this paper is that sufficient evidence has been accumulated to show that both quantum physics and Einstein's two great theories are now, if not false, at least inadequate to the facts and hence if science is to be true to its ideals, the theories themselves must be either radically modified or replaced. Because we are dealing with foundational issues – properly the concern of metascience - I think it necessary to emphasize that science itself evolves, and that observation must ultimately take precedence over theory, however elegant may be its mathematical formulation. T. H. Huxley famously said that "the great tragedy of science is that it must allow a beautiful theory to be slain by an ugly fact," but I would differ from him in saying this sort of intellectual honesty and open-mindedness is not a tragedy but a mark of the nobility of science. In the end, it separates the true scientists from those who may identify themselves as scientists and wear the word as a badge, but whose horizon of curiosity is narrow and whose unquestioning commitment to orthodoxy marks them out not as truth-seekers but as camp-followers.

In arguing for a post-Einsteinian approach to science one is necessarily probing into new philosophical and theological paradigms, and this paper, which began as a half hour presentation can do little more than highlight the main postulates and indicate some of the empirical evidence which gives them initial justification. Of these postulates the most important are:

- that hyperspace is a real reality
- that the photon is a point particle
- that the cosmos originated as a dimensionless point of energy.

Together these provide a conceptual keystone locking into place new paradigms in both science and theology.

The Disorientation of the New

Before embarking on the main subject, a few words should perhaps be said about the nature of new paradigms. Thomas Kuhn, who introduced the term "paradigm" in the sense of a constellation of fundamental scientific principles, came eventually to regret it, because it so rapidly became trivialized. One hears the word all around - new paradigm in retailing, new paradigm in hairdressing, etc. - but Kuhn's original point was that for scientists a new paradigm is a cognitive revolution, and usually very disturbing for this reason. As the cultural psychologist Anthony Storr says, "Any form of new organization or integration within the mind has to be preceded by some degree of disorganization. No one can tell, until he has experienced it, whether or not this necessary disruption of former patterns will be succeeded by something better."[1] Kuhn compared the effect of accepting a new paradigm to a religious conversion, and the astronomer Celia Payne-Gaposchkin said that her first encounter with Einstein's General Relativity (at a talk given by Eddington) was to bring on for a few days something like a nervous breakdown. The disorientating effects of a new scientific paradigm should not be surprising, nor the similarity of its acceptance to a religious conversion, for genuine scientific and theological paradigms both involve change in our assumptions about the nature of reality. It is, indeed, possible that after the initial shock of discovery, new neural circuitry may be required to fully comprehend the significance of a genuinely new paradigm. The "genuinely new" may be recognized in the fact that it offers – and demands – either or both a new epistemology or ontology.

Science Needs a New Epistemology

Empirical science is founded very consciously on direct and experimental observation, and initially on the assumption that the eye records "facts" like a camera before transmitting them to the brain. This assumption has been comprehensively destroyed by a wide variety of findings, though it still exercises a powerful hold, and must indeed be taken as a starting point in science. We know, for instance, that what we call "light" is only that frequency band of electromagnetic vibration that is within the visible spectrum, but very rarely is it considered that the darkest room is filled with invisible light. Nearly fifty years ago there appeared a now classical paper on perceptual neurology, entitled "What the Frog's Eye Tells the Frog's Brain,"[2] which reported on experiments that showed dramatically that the optical system is far from being a direct recording of a reality "out there". In over-simple summary, what the experiment found was that the retina of the frogs in question saw only grey and white bands, and when something small moved across the field, the frog's tongue was triggered to shoot out and catch it. This was reality for the frog.

It takes no great imagination to suppose that the human eye similarly evolved to ensure physical survival, and that it too offers the brain a limited perception of reality. This being so, a science based on naive realism – i.e., the simple camera analogy - will be critically defective; it will contain inherent contradictions from the start which will eventually break the theory apart. Science is sometimes described as systematized commonsense, but it may equally be regarded as a systematic attempt to go beyond common sense - that is, beyond the limits of sense perception - in order to gain a truer understanding of reality. What the brain receives is, so to speak, raw sense data which has been systematically interpreted through a learned process until the interpretation is taken to be part of the act of seeing. The retina of the eye is, for instance, a two-dimensional array of receptors which processes incoming light signals through the optic nerve and the brain converts them to give us a three-dimensional awareness. In the process it uses visual clues, such as shadows and highlights, in cooperation with stereoscopic vision, to reach the conclusion that an object is three-dimensional. The end-result is that a few months after birth we have <u>learned</u> to see the world as three-dimensional by a seamless process of direct vision and logical inference.

Perhaps the greatest challenge facing science today is how we are to raise our inferential powers to a new level in order to reach a better understanding of reality as hyperspatial. This will need to be a very conscious process, as against the unconscious way in which we learn to see a three-dimensional world. As physical science progresses, it goes further from its initial empirical ideals, and as cosmology becomes cosmogony science finds itself uncomfortably on ground that once was considered the preserve of theology. For this reason, and to clarify the situation post-Hubble, a dual definition of science now needs to be considered, and I will make some initial comments below on what I have called *philoscience* and *technoscience* to draw attention to the differences.

Physics Needs a New Ontology

Roger Penrose has called Einsteinian Relativity "the most beautiful and self-contained of physical theories".[3] It has dominated physical science for eighty years, and anything which is proposed as a replacement will have to go down to the very foundations of science itself. In John Wheeler's words, "If we are ever going to find an element of nature that explains space and time, we surely have to find something that is deeper than space or time - something that itself has no localization in space or time,"[4] and ontology, the philosophical discipline which deals with reality, is the natural place to begin the search.

Einstein's reality was the three-dimensional realm and *res extensa* which Descartes had proposed as the basis of what was then the new kind of knowledge - *nuova scienza*, as Galileo and Vico had called it. Cartesianism did not necessarily rule out the existence of other kinds of reality, though some scientists believe this to be the case, but merely restricts genuine science to what is in principle observable and measurable. Reasons for questioning Cartesian orthodoxy had been building up for fifty years before Einstein's revolutionary thinking pushed it to its explanatory limits. In a two year space between 1843 and 1845 Hamilton, Grassman, Cayley and Clifford all published pioneering work on the mathematics of 3 + dimensions. Nine years later Riemann's multi-dimensional geometry appeared, and in 1874 Cantor's theory of transfinite sets. However, and as always, the ontological question was, is this multidimensionality real in some objective sense or merely within the mind of the mathematicians?

Since Einstein published his General Theory of Relativity in 1915, a great deal of disconnected physical evidence for the existence of something other than 3-space has started to appear, and the general idea of hyperspace has become familiar, partly through science fiction. It seems, in fact, that physics has been pushing up against a conceptual barrier through which it cannot break, despite a variety of initiatives to model the "potentials without a field" that Maxwell claimed on the basis of quaternion analysis. In the 1873 first edition of *A Treatise on Electricity and Magnetism* he asserted that "There are physical quantities of another kind which are related to directions in space, which are not vectors [but] are expressed in the language of quaternions by linear and vector functions of a vector." In very different guises these more-than-three dimensional quantities (or, rather perhaps, operators) have reappeared more recently in such initiatives as David Bohm's hidden variable theory, later given experimental support in the Aharonov-Bohm Effect, string theory, the Berry phase and Everett's many universes theory. It would be inappropriate to attempt even the sketchiest review of the literature here, but it is perhaps worth noting that string theory, which is the nearest thing to current orthodoxy in physical theory, rests on multi-dimensional resonances billions of times smaller than the proton. Also worth noting is that Lee Smolin, once the acknowledged leader in the field of string theory, and its offshoot loop quantum gravity, has called for its abandonment in his 2006 book, *The Trouble with Physics*. "What I believe is failing," he says, "is not so much a particular theory but a style of doing science that was well suited to the problems we faced in the past." We need to return, he argues, to "the way that the early-twentieth century revolutionaries did science. Their work arose from deep thought on the most basic questions surrounding space, time and matter, and they saw what they did as part of a broader philosophical tradition in which they were at home." [5]

The first great challenge is to accept the existence of hyperspace as a valid concept in physics, a scientific reality, even though it is inaccessible to the senses, and thus fails the test of scientific empiricism. Once that is accepted as either a postulate, an axiom or hypothesis (the difference is important), the second challenge is to decide whether hyperspace (as yet undefined) exists within Cartesian 3-space, as do solid objects, or whether, on the contrary, 3-space is contained in some sense within hyperspace. String theory is typical in assuming that multidimensional reality exists within our familiar 3-space, but this Cartesian assumption blinds us to the possibility that in order to advance, science needs to turn the common world view inside out, and approach the cosmos, huge as it may be, as a subspace of a higher invisible reality. Once that step is taken, the whole nature of physical science must start to change.

Some influential theorists are aware of this and expressly resist it, most notably perhaps Stephen Hawking, who is explicit in *A Brief History of Time* that his theorizing is strictly within a three-dimensional reality. Once 3-space is defined as within hyperspace, physics moves not only into post-Einsteinian science but into post-Cartesian science. It is then faced with the task of formalizing the concept and finding (or creating?) mathematical expression. Maxwell, interestingly, came at the problem from the other side, seeking to understand a higher reality from the mathematical existence of Hamilton's quaternions.

Empirical Science and Faith in Things Unseen

Science, which is based on observable knowledge, underwent a crisis with the publication in 1808 of John Dalton's publication *New System of Chemical Philosophy*. In this pioneering work, which was written when science was regarded as a particular branch of philosophy, Dalton put forward the theory that matter was composed of indivisible particles of measurable mass and properties that made them combine in certain proportions. This first proposal of modern atomic theory was widely accepted by chemists for its practical value, but resisted by theoretical physicists because these notional atoms were too small to be seen. The two most famous objectors were Ernst Mach, perhaps the most eminent philosopher of science in his time, and Wilhelm Ostwald, the Nobel Laureate chemist, who refused to accept the empirical reality of the atom, considering it no more than "a mathematical fiction." It was not until 1903, with the invention of the sphinthariscope, and only two years before Einstein's Special Relativity Theory, that Mach conceded. (The sphinthariscope registered radioactive particles as flashes on a fluorescent screen.) As Hans Christian von Bayer tells the story, "Mach's assistants dragged the sixty-five-year-old doubting Thomas to witness this marvel, which represented visible evidence for the reality of atoms. Mach squinted into the apparatus, saw the scintillations and surrendered. 'Now I believe in the existence of the atom,' he said." [6]

A similar crisis is being replayed today, but without hope that new instrumentation will provide a clear cut resolution, for we cannot reach into the invisible realm of the zero point energy vacuum, the proton or the Big Bang event, which is where the great issues of physics today lie. However, Einstein himself led the way towards a methodology that will allow progress to be made, for his systematic use of the thought-experiment and the postulational method together constitute a radical extension of the principles of hypothetical-inductive science. An even more radical extension is now required to take physics and cosmology forward.

The Importance of Hubble

Since Hubble's discovery of the galactic redshift, science has faced a similar challenge to its empirical basis as it did after Dalton, and the great majority of scientists, like Mach and Ostwald in an earlier age, are unwilling to accept the validity of proof drawn from theoretical coherence, though many see proof in mathematical elegance. From observation of the redshift it can be inferred that we live in an expanding cosmos made up of billions of galaxies, structured in clusters and sub-clusters, separated by "walls" of empty space and orbiting over vast periods of time.

There is every reason to think that the basic Hubble theory is in need of drastic revision, with observational data suggesting that the redshift may have more than one cause, and may be age-related as well as velocity related, as Halton Arp first proposed. The so-called Plasma Universe theory, as argued by Eric Lerner and others, presents strong evidence that galactic attraction may be magnetic as well as gravitational, and Ernest Sternglass's revival of Lemaitre's theory of the cosmic atom and John Gribbin's theory of White Holes all demand serious attention, although none are mainstream cosmology. From a historical perspective, it may well prove to be that these new models, together or in part, will give definitive correction to the simple model of an expanding universe, as Kepler's data-based theory of elliptical orbits corrected Copernicus's simple and "obvious" model which assumed that all the heavenly bodies moved in circular orbits.

In any event, when Einstein produced his Special Theory of Relativity in 1905, it was almost universally believed that the universe consisted only of our galaxy, although Kant had (quite astonishingly) proposed about 1750 that certain "nebulosities", visible to the naked eye, were not glowing stars but other galactic worlds reduced by distance to near-point size. The multiple galaxy speculation was confirmed in the early twentieth century by astronomers working with new and more powerful telescopes, especially by Leavitt and Slipher. Even then, however, it was assumed that however many galaxies the universe might contain, it was just sitting there, as it had done from all eternity. The alternative, that the universe had come into existence at a definite time in the past, seems never to have been considered (except by theologians) even when Einstein's original field equations pointed towards that possibility. As is well known, he deliberately excluded this hypothesis by inserting his notorious cosmological constant to justify his belief that the universe was of a fixed size and eternal. This was a perfectly reasonable postulate, since there was at that time no evidence from astronomy that anything was expanding and absolutely no reason to believe that it was, even though we take it so totally for granted today. Friedmann's 1922 theory did lead to the conclusion that the universe began as a point of matter (or, rather, of energy), but was hardly more than a mathematical conjecture until Hubble provided the physical evidence. It is hard for us today to imagine how mind-blowing was the thought of an expanding universe at that time, so much so that even Hubble himself was initially reluctant to draw this conclusion from his data.

With the benefit of hindsight, Einstein's cosmological constant can be seen as one of three fudge factors which enabled his thinking to stay within the framework of Cartesian science. The second fudge is his invention (with Minkowski) of spacetime, by means of which objects could be given, as it were, an extra dimension, without going all the way into the potentially infinite dimensions of Riemannian geometry. Einsteinian spacetime is a halfway house, reminiscent of Tycho Brahe's half-heliocentric universe, in which all the planets orbited the sun, except the earth, which retained its centrality in the great scheme of things. Space-time is undevelopable because to call time a dimension is a confusion of physical categories which offers specious benefits but soon loses its apparent value.

The constant speed of light in a vacuum can be seen as a third fudge, insofar as it does not supply the absolutely fixed point of reference demanded by Einstein's own (and Galileo's) principles of the relativity of motion. Einstein is curiously ambivalent here, for while he emphasized that the perception of motion depends on a fixed observer, he seems to have overlooked the fact that fixity itself is relative. That is to say, one cannot be sure that anything at all is fixed without having some other fixed point, or frame, as a referent. Thus we seem to enter into a problem of infinite regression, since determining whether any reference point is fixed demands another fixed point, and so on *ad infinitum*. Ultimately one must define the speed of light as fixed in relation to something else, and Lorentz invariance only answers the question partially. Simple logic would seem to lead to the conclusion that if an infinite regression of reference coordinates is rejected, the fixed viewpoint that is essential to science requires either an infinite number of potential observers or a single hypothesized universal observer. The latter would be hardly distinguishable from the Unmoved Mover of Aristotelian metaphysics, and too close for comfort to the Christian idea of God.

Newton's insistence that science can only be science by excluding occult forces as an explanation is perhaps the most unquestionable of scientific principles, but this principle is now causing great strains in science and undermining the even greater principle of honesty before the facts. The problem is how to deal with evidence for the existence of factors or forces that cannot be observed and handled experimentally. This is a particularly acute problem for evolutionary biology, which has until now been handled very badly, essentially by going into corporate denial. The Central Dogma (revealing term!) of what is called "the new synthesis" of Darwinism, Mendelism and molecular biology routinely sweeps away by diktat evidence for design, simply by calling it "apparent evidence." This surely is to degrade science and create a new kind of closed-minded fundamentalism. Genuine science does not ignore observational evidence in order to fit an existing theory but, if necessary, goes back to re-examine the theory. As T.H. Huxley often asserted, the true scientist "sits down before the facts like a child."

Physics has never been affected by the design problem that plagues biology, for without compromising their principles, physicists both theistic and atheistic could assume that the universe was a self-contained machine which could be understood without any reference to its designer. Since Hubble, however, our knowledge that we live in an expanding universe has led inevitably to questions about how it all began, and to a crisis in science, leaving it with two impossible alternatives. On the assumption that time and space came into existence at the point of the Big Bang, the trigger for cosmic expansion is held to be an occult force or, following Hawking, a quantum fluctuation. The latter, however, is a logical impossibility, since a fluctuation is only possible in time and space, and we are seeking here a cause for the emergence of time and space. Edward Tryon, who coined the phrase quantum fluctuation, was quite open about the fact that it has no explanatory power at all, saying, "In answer to the question of why it happened, I offer the modest proposal that our Universe is simply one of those things which happen from time to time." This is no better than the "God of the gaps" answer which is, rightly, ridiculed in science, and it would be far better for science in general to be honest and say simply that we do not know. There is, however, a legitimate case for arguing that the trigger was a conscious act of a hypothesized power (whether or not we may wish to call it "occult") completely analogous to the way in which a bio-physical event, such as lifting a weight, happens through a chain of muscular changes of chemical and electromagnetic origin, which is triggered by a conscious will to lift it. Without this initial act of will nothing happens. Almost all contemporary scientists find such an analogy unacceptable, not because of any inherent illogic but because to accept it would seem to let in occult forces and destroy science itself or, more accurately, science as we presently understand it.

Adjustments to Einstein's Special Relativity

In the past half century new discoveries about the nature of light and of apparently empty space have put the principle of Special Relativity in question, but without producing any alternative. These include Sagnac's experimental proof in 1913 that light travels at different speeds in clockwise and anti-clockwise rotation, Casimir's discovery in 1948 of the force named after him (refined experimentally by Lamoureaux in 1997), and two more recent discoveries whose significance has not yet entered into mainstream physics, namely that

- the speed of light is not a constant, but can be manipulated downwards experimentally, essentially by lowering the temperature of the ambient space.

- light travels not in waves but through helical propagation of the photon

The first fact about light travel was discovered by Lene Hau[7] and other teams in the late 1990's, essentially by passing focused light through the near zero temperature of a Bose-Einstein condensate. Under the simple statement are experiments of great precision, elegance and perseverance, in which a stream of photons was slowed down and eventually frozen into stillness, earning Hau the title of "the ringmaster of light." The significance of these experimental results has hardly impacted yet on mainstream physics, perhaps because it is sensed that to accept them would eventually bring the need for a total overhaul of Einstein's Special Relativity.

It is, for instance, reasonable to deduce from them that in the early period of cosmic expansion, when the temperature would have been measured in billions of degrees, light travelled at extremely high speeds, and if this is the case, then Einstein's constant, C, would actually vary in relation to the energy density of the cosmos at different stages of its expansion, and would thus be a special case of a more general theory. There is without doubt an upper limit to the velocity of light at the 300,000 km/sec, which, it would seem, is a barrier that prevents three dimensional entities being compressed to two dimensions, "pancaked," to use Richard Feynman's graphic term. This leads to further speculation, for example whether some short-lived particles created in accelerators are actually two dimensional. Is it, for instance, possible that the muon is an electron in 2D? Another anomaly worth pointing out is that C is the speed of light in a *vacuum*, a condition which does not exist in nature, and thus the measurement of the velocity of light in the famous experiment of Michelson and Morley seems not to be relevant to Einstein's C.

The converse of the experimentally proven fact that light decelerates in low ambient temperatures would seem *prima facie* to add weight to Alan Guth's hypothesis that the cosmos expanded at an incredibly rapid rate in the first fraction of a second after it came into existence. Given intense radiation pressure at the moment of the Big Bang, there is every reason to think that light propagated, and the cosmos expanded, at an exceptional rate. However, the logic of this deduction appears to be contradicted by recent findings that the speed of the expansion of the cosmos is actually increasing. These few facts would be sufficient to revisit Einstein's Special Relativity, and there are other related issues that have never been adequately addressed, such as what kind of domain the 3D cosmos is expanding into, and what exactly was the size of the point of the Big Bang at its inception.[8]

The second experimental finding which calls Special Relativity into question - namely, that what we call a light ray is actually a photon travelling in a helical path - seems to have been first proposed by J. L Gaasenbeek[9] but appears as an assumption elsewhere in the use of optical fibre technology,[10] and may have been an idea "in the air," since experiments in circularly polarized light, fibre optic and co-axial cable technology had raised awareness that more general laws of light propagation were at work. R. A. Ashworth has dealt with the phenomenon of helical light travel as it appears in waveguide technology.[11]

These few references stand out as anomalies in current theory, and, so far as I can see, no attempt has been made to coordinate them in search of a more general theory about the nature of light and its propagation. My modest contribution to this is a suggestion that photon travel is not strictly helical but vortical. Without giving an extended justification for this conclusion, it is worth noting that experimental work on fibre optics and waveguides are on a scale where the vortical approximates to the helical without any loss of accuracy or significance. However, in extrapolating to the cosmic scale, an assumed vortical propagation would be compatible with the spatial expansion of the cosmos and with the dilution of energy that goes along with it. Much more theorizing, and perhaps an *experimentum crucis*, will be required to develop this growing complex of new ideas about the nature of light into a full blown new physical paradigm. Large scale thinking is now required to bring together quantum physics and cosmology. In the words of David Lindley, a former associate editor of Nature, "Full understanding of the fundamental particles and forces or of the birth of the universe will be achieved ... only through a long and indirect chain of reasoning from what happened a long time ago, under circumstances we can barely imagine, to what is before us now."[12]

The Photon as Particle

Before Hubble, questions about the emergence in time of particle types did not enter into physics, now they are unavoidable. Physics, through cosmology, has become a historical discipline. In fact, both are now so symbiotic that it is high time a single new word was coined to recognize this fact, and it might be worthwhile to resurrect Ostwald's term *energetics* to indicate that both fields are now coming at the same question of what might be called "configurations of energy" but from different directions.

Be that as it may, the casual use of imprecise, everyday words to label very precise, and controversial aspects of energy conformation has led physics into a cul de sac. Such critical concepts as *moment, instant, particle, matter, mass* and, indeed *energy* itself, on which the whole of physics depends, reveal upon examination logical fuzziness and contradictions. Nearly eighty years ago Niels Bohr drew attention to the way in which the vision of physics is blinkered by loose terminology, "We find ourselves," he said, "on the path ... of adapting our modes of perception to the gradually deepening knowledge of the laws of Nature [and] the hindrances met on this path originate above all in the fact that, so to say, every word in the language refers to our ordinary perception."[13]

Nowhere is this looseness of terminology more obvious than in the word *particle*, and when it comes to the photon, the confusion is compounded because the principle that light is both wave and particle has become almost a mantra, inhibiting further effort to understand why this should be so. To put the problem in the context of the present essay, if a light ray is a photon travelling in a helical path, as has been experimentally proven, what sort of thing is the photon that is travelling?

Since it has never, apparently, been suggested that the photon has an internal structure, I would propose that the only alternative to Newton's belief that a structureless particle must be solid and unbreakable is that it must be a point. More specifically, it must be a point of energy, a particular instance of the point charge which is a commonplace in electrical theory. If the photon is taken to be an oscillating point charge, three questions immediately arise - what is the origin of the energy which is located at that point, what force makes it oscillate, and is the oscillation in one, two or three dimensions?

The implications of postulating the helical travel of the photon call for a treatise, but two may be selected here for their immediate significance. Firstly, the photon must travel in two different ways and at two quite different speeds, namely along the axis of the helix and around its circumference. With suitable qualifications, what Einstein considered to be the speed of light may be taken as the axial speed, and this may be considered normally to be the constant *c*. The angular momentum of the photon is of more immediate interest for several reasons, not least because if the visualized helix is sectioned lengthwise, thus giving a two-dimensional representation of a three-dimensional reality, the travel of photon will appear as the peaks and troughs of a sine wave, which is, of course, the usual 2D representation of the 3D electromagnetic wave. The imagined cylinder is a volume not of energy but of action, and its action density can be thought of as something like a coiled spring which can vary in proportion to its length. The fact that it is clearly action density would suggest that there exists, as Maxwell suspected, a kind of timeless energy, which is usually acknowledged in the term *scalar potential*.

Abandonment of General Relativity

Whereas Special Relativity is a theory that needs to be reconsidered in the light of new knowledge, General Relativity is essentially a point of observation which cannot be adjusted but must be abandoned entirely if a more revealing point is found. In this sense the revolution that Einstein started with General Relativity, though usually set against Newtonian theory, is actually more comparable in its limitations to Ptolemy's model of the earth-centred universe. After the Copernicus-Kepler model was given to the world, astronomers and scientists more generally were faced with an either-or choice, and a similar moment of decision is approaching again. Is the metacentre of the universe to be taken as within our galaxy – as Einstein assumed - or is it the Big Bang point, or does science go even further? Is cosmology now being called to observe the universe itself from "outside", as it were, that is to say, as a huge three-dimensional domain within the multi-dimensioned hyperspace where it began its existence as a dimensionless point of unimaginable energy? This would be a new Copernicanism, and whatever the answer may turn out to be, the new vantage point must be chosen only because it leads to a better scientific theory, as once Copernicus's heliocentric model of the cosmos proved its superiority to the geocentric model of Ptolemy.

A better theory must

- be conceptually simpler than the theory it replaces
- offer an explanation of the universe without contradictions
- rest upon a minimum of special or arbitrary postulates

- lead to conclusions, which are testable, at least in theory
- make new predictions
- be mathematically coherent,
- be more comprehensive.

On several of these counts it is recognized that General Relativity has grave weaknesses. It is incompatible with quantum physics, the mathematics is over-complex (space exploration can, for instance, function perfectly well with the simpler Newtonian model), and while it has had some predictive successes, these can by achieved by other models, based on different premises.

Peter Coles has listed five questions now facing cosmological theory, none of which can be answered by General Relativity, namely,

- What was the nature of the early universe?
- Is the universe finite or infinite?
- What is dark energy?
- What is dark matter?
- Did inflation really happen?

Einstein's General Relativity can answer none of these, and is comprehensively deficient in that it is no longer a general theory. It is, in Coles' words, "essentially local and provides no prescription for the large-scale connectivity of space."[14]

General Relativity's initial, and continuing, claim to acceptance is that it offers an explanation for the origin of gravity which is absent from Newton's purely descriptive theory, which was justified by its predictiveness. Newton conceded that the origin of universal gravitation was a total mystery, and he was not even going to guess - *hypotheses non fingo*. By contrast, Einstein claimed to have found the source of gravity in an inherent tension within space, itself the consequence of time and space being curved by the presence of matter. It is quite astonishing how the tautologous nature of this explanation has been overlooked from the beginning, for it actually assumes what it sets out to prove, namely, that massive bodies exert a distorting gravitational force on the "fabric" of space-time, without giving any explanation of how mass acquired this force in the first place. One can only conclude that General Relativity took over physics by default, simply because there was at the time no other causal explanation of any kind for universal gravitation. Since Hubble there has been one waiting in the wings, but several factors have combined to delay its entrance, the most important perhaps being perhaps the inertial effect of the Einsteinian paradigm.

Technoscience and Philoscience

"Science" is a noble but ambiguous word, and I return now to the issue mentioned earlier of the need for disambiguation. I would propose that there are two kinds of science , the first practical, which is an adjunct to technology on every scale, and the second a type of understanding, from which the scientific attitude develops, and which comes from appreciating science as a truth system. Though related at some deep level, there are good reasons for considering them as separate disciplines. The sad fact is that few scientists are actually interested in science itself - its origins, its evolution, its status as a truth system or as a reliable measure of reality. Their horizons tend to be bounded by the specific scientific problem with which they are engaged, and the philosophical element is well outside their professional concerns. With this as background, I have coined the word "technoscience" to refer to that aspect of scientific method which is appropriate to technology, and "philoscience" to that aspect which overlaps with philosophy, a word whose root meaning is "love of wisdom."

Science itself was long known as "natural philosophy", and my proposal is really no more than a continuation of the debate that William Whewell opened in 1833, when he proposed the neologism "scientist" to replace "natural philosopher" as an identifying term for those who sought truth by the hypothetico-inductive method. Not all his readers liked the new term, thinking it either redundant or imprecise. Maxwell, for instance, preferred to call himself an "electrician", to signify the new direction that natural philosophy had taken, and some, like Ostwald, as already noted, wanted physics to be renamed "energetics" – a term which, as noted above, I think needs to be dusted off. I mention these historical facts as evidence that science does evolve and that new perceptions call for newly invented words. Until technoscience and philoscience are clearly distinguished, there is scope for endless misunderstanding, and particularly where science and theology interface. I think it would, in fact, be accurate to say that technoscience does not interface with theology at all, and, if this is so, those bodies which attempt to harmonise science and religion should be clearly aware of the dangers lurking in the ambiguity of the single word "science".

References

1. Anthony Storr, *Solitude*. London: Harper Collins, 1988. p. 35

2. J. Y. Lettwin, H. R. Maturana, W. S. McCulloch, W. H. Pitts, "What the Frog's Eye Tells the Frog's Brain", *Proc. Inst. Eng.* 47, 1959, 1940-51. Reprinted in Warren S. McCulloch, *Embodiments of Mind*. MIT Press, 1965.

3. In the preface to Richard Feynman's *Six Not So Easy Pieces: Einstein's Relativity, Symmetry and Space-Time*. London: Allen Lane, 1997 [1963]

4. John Wheeler, in P.C.W. Davies and J.R. Brown (eds.), *The Ghost in the Atom*. CÚP, 2000 [1986], p. 66.

5. Lee Smolin, *The Trouble with Physics*. New York: Houghton Mifflin, 2006. p. xxii.

6. Hans Christian von Bayer, *Taming the Atom: The Emergence of the Visible Microworld*. New York: Viking, 1992, p.18.

7. Lene Hau, "Frozen Light," *Scientific American* 285, 52-55 (July 2001)

8. These issues are addressed systematically in my forthcoming *Neoscience* (publication planned for autumn 2010).

9. J. L. Gaasenbeek, (cf. "Foundation for proposed Theorems of Relativity," *Speculations in Science and Technology*, Vol. 9, No. 4, 1986.)

10. Tomita and Chiao seem to have taken it for granted in experimental work verifying the Berry phase ("Observation of Berry's Topological Phase by Use of an Optical Fiber," *Phys. Rev. Lett.* 57, 937-940, 1986).

11. R. A. Ashworth, "Confirmation of Helical Light Travel Through Microwave Waveguide Analysis," *Physics Essays*, Vol. 11, No. 3, 1998.

12. David Lindley, *The End of Physics: The Myth of a Unified Theory*. London: Basic Books, 1995, p. 156.

13. Niels Bohr, *Nature* (Supplement) April, 14, 1928, p. 580.

14. Peter Coles, "The State of the Universe," news@nature.com 19.1.2005.

DARWIN CONTRA DARWINISM

What would Darwin have made of neo-Darwinism, which is his original theory brought up to date with molecular biology and genetics? On the surface, all the evidence provided by the additions seems to reinforce his theory that biological evolution could be explained by the simple principle of natural selection or, to use Huxley's phrase, survival of the fittest. So much is this the case that Darwinism and neo-Darwinism are usually treated as synonymous for all practical purposes. In the context of survival, the term "fittest" does not, of course, mean healthiest, but the most adaptable to a given environment, and Darwin's argument was that over enormous periods of time, and in the most minute particulars, organisms and whole species would survive or die out as slight changes in each generation enabled them to adapt or otherwise. Nature in this view reveals a world of climatic and environmental niches which have been filled by creatures with a quite astonishing power to adapt, such as the archaea which can live comfortably at boiling temperatures in a strongly acid environment, dining happily on a diet of sulphur.

Darwin's theory of natural selection was his second great imaginative leap, the first being the "tree of life," a vivid representation of the thesis that all living organisms were descended from a common primitive ancestor which had evolved and branched over billions of years. In conjunction with genetic determinism, natural selection has become the Central Dogma of what is called the New Synthesis. The Central Dogma, as the term would suggest, is a matter of belief and it is of great interest that few professional biologists would even think it open to question, whereas Darwin proposed it as a theory which, like any other scientific theory, had to be tested against the evidence. If it could be proved right, then biology had found the grail of all the sciences, a machine model from which predictions could be made with absolute certainty. But if, on the contrary, evidence turned up that could not be explained by the theory, biologists would be facing their worst nightmare. If a deterministic theory did not explain the facts, there would seem to be no alternative to calling in Newton's "occult forces" or the religionists' "god of the gaps." There was a great deal at stake, and not just in biology, for the way in which the evidence was handled and interpreted would be a test case for scientific integrity.

Darwin himself was religiously agnostic, though initially a Christian believer. His loss of faith seems to have been a gradual process, but since he did not write specifically about it (except sometimes in private correspondence), we can only speculate on its causes. It is perfectly possible that thinking as a scientist led to rejection of the mythological basis of Christianity, and this in turn weakened his belief in a supreme power of any kind, but it is equally probable that he simply saw keeping an explanatory god out of science as a moral principle.[1] He is sometimes wrongly called an atheist, but everything we know about him suggests that he would have listed himself as a "Don't Know". He seems to have regretted his loss of religious faith, but it did not have any bearing on his theory of the mechanism of evolution, which he approached in a thoroughly scientific fashion, as a theory to be tested and proved before acceptance, and possibly needing radical modification. In *The Origin of Species*, he says quite categorically:

> *If it could be demonstrated that any complex organ existed which could not possibly have been formed by numerous, successive, slight modifications, my theory would absolutely break down.*

This is precisely what the microbiologist Michael Behe set out to demonstrate in his best-selling *Darwin's Black Box: The Biochemical Challenge to Evolution* (1996), and this is where one might wonder how Darwin would have reacted when confronted with the evidence against simple Darwinism that the book set out to provide. The book is still regularly cited as evidence for either the existence of a design factor in evolution or, on the other hand, as a particularly gross example of bad science, warped by religious prejudice. The disinterested observer must surely conclude that one or other of these judgements must be wrong, or perhaps both, but the philosopher of evolution will ask how it is possible for people of intelligence and integrity to reach such opposite conclusions. The answer has to be more a matter of psychology than of either religion or science.

The black box in the title of Behe's book is the "molecular machine" of the cell, and his argument was that the degree of complexity which is revealed at this level is so great that it cannot *in principle* have evolved merely through natural selection. Thus he believed that Darwin's theory of natural selection, though sound in outline, is incomplete, and possibly a special theory within a more general theory yet to appear. He does not say it is wrong, only that it cannot be invoked as a universal explanation of how evolution has happened. The complexity of which Behe writes concerns not just the internal arrangement of the cell, but the way in which its subsystems must have come together in time to make it function. From data which is not disputed, he concludes that chance alone cannot account for the combination of these molecular subsystems happening with such exquisite timing and in complex sequencing. Take away "chance and necessity" as the all-embracing explanation of current evolutionary orthodoxy and, he argued, the internal workings of the cell point inexorably to a design or purposive factor of some unknown kind. The intensity of opposition to Behe's book is such as to indicate that there is something more than biological fact involved in this dispute, and that the New Synthesis has become, for whatever reason, an act of faith that does not admit of questioning.

Behe's scientific case actually received less than justice from both religious and scientific camps, for fundamentalist Christians seized upon it to justify their belief in the literal truth of the Bible, which Behe would not have accepted, while professional biologists reacted with varying degrees of "Oh no, not that old chestnut again!" One reviewer dismissed it as "just the latest, and no doubt not the last, attempt to put God back into nature", accused the author of "falling back on the old, limp idea of 'design'" and warned readers "not to be fooled."[2] Another opens with, "What is so sad about this book is that the author thinks he ... is contributing to science," and in general castigates Behe for "being ignorant of evolutionary biology" and of "using "the empty, religious notion of intelligent design" and "intellectually dishonest double standards." The same reviewer grudgingly admits to finding "relatively few factual errors" (having actually mentioned none at all), but suspects that "as a Catholic, Behe prefers the illusion of an intelligent biochemist creator to mutations and the blind gropings of macro-molecules."[3] This is despite Behe's argument that the facts are so compelling that they leave no room for preference, whatever one's temperament or religious bias. Indeed, this is the whole point of the book.

This broadside of personal insults – "empty, ignorant, dishonest, limp, sad" - is the very antithesis of science. It is no better than the *odium theologicum* that has disfigured religious debate over the centuries, and it has the same cause – a determination not to question or allow questioning of issues where tribal self-identity is involved. This is a cause for shame among true scientists, and everything we know about Darwin suggests that he would weep at the sad state to which "Darwinism" has sunk. We have here for most professional biologists a crossroads of personal honesty.

Behe's argument that cell function cannot be fully explained without recourse to some design factor poses an acute dilemma for biology: does the "irreducible complexity" of the cell at molecular level compel a radical extension or revision of accepted orthodoxy? The great challenge to scientific integrity, it has been said, is to "allow an ugly fact to kill a beautiful theory", but we are dealing here not just with a theory but with the keystone of a whole scientific paradigm, and that will make resistance to the "ugly fact" all the stronger. Behe's argument may or may not convince, but it adds significantly to other evidence that neo-Darwinism is becoming "no more nor less than the great cosmogenic myth of the Twentieth Century".[4] Neo-Darwinism - natural selection combined with mechanical gene replication and random mutation - is unquestionably a beautiful theory: it is powerful, simple, elegant and productive - the very ideal of science. Its explanatory power has been continually reinforced by new discoveries which have demonstrated the astonishing things that a blindly winnowing nature can "create", so much so that any evidence of design is now routinely dismissed, one might even say "exorcised", by calling it "apparent design", thus in effect making the theory invulnerable to disproof. In this regard, it is worth recalling that Karl Popper based the whole value of scientific theorising on the fact that it is vulnerable to disproof. Saying this, however, takes the philosopher of science to a deeper, and murkier, level where the nature of proof needs to be established, and the reasons why prejudice or fear so often overcome logic and observation.

Paradoxically, the explanatory and predictive power of Darwinism can become a weakness insofar as it gives valid reason for not giving proper attention to counter-evidence, since *prima facie*, and in good faith, such counter-evidence is assumed to contain flaws of some kind. Delay and caution are an understandable response from professional biologists when a theory so powerful as neo-Darwinism is called into question, but this can become a Catch 22, for it generates a subtle temptation to call for more faith and for patience, *ad infinitum*. Insensibly this can become in practice a principled refusal to examine unwelcome data on its merits.

Darwin's theory of natural selection was greatly influenced by his observation of the selective breeding of farm animals which had become a practical science in the eighteenth century. When random genetic mutation was later shown to be a biological fact, it seemed that the ability of an organism first to change, and then for its descendents to self-select for survival and multiply could explain how the evolutionary process could be selective without invoking a quasi-human will. In fact, the theory of evolutionary change now hinges so critically upon random mutation that it has become the scientific equivalent of the religionist's "god of the gaps." Max Delbrück, a co-founder of molecular biology and Nobel Laureate, once wryly remarked that

DNA had become for biologists what the unmoved mover was for Aristotle and mediaeval philosophers.

What would Darwin think, if he were alive today, of counter-evidence to random and mechanical mutation as a universal explanation for change? There is growing awareness, for example, that genetic transcription is not fully machine-like, but is critically affected by nutrition and the complex chemistry of the environment.[5] The clearest "black swan," however, revealing exceptions to the determinism of the Central Dogma, is without doubt the now classic experiment of John Cairns and associates, which showed how bacteria can mutate for survival not randomly but with a purpose when conditions change.[6] This finding was at first as unwelcome as Behe's irreducible complexity, but to the credit of biologists, it has not been buried. The original experiment has been replicated, and honest attempts have been made to interpret the data in a non-purposive form.[7] Without collating the literature, the present position appears to be something of a standoff.

As regards Darwin's complementary theory of "the tree of life," which is more foundational even than natural selection, and more powerful, discoveries over the past twenty years are calling for modifications so radical as to cast doubt on the core perception. Even worse (or better!), they are casting doubt on the value of the basic taxonomy on which the whole science of evolutionary biology is based, and not least on the concept of species, which is found to be so rubbery in some areas, especially bacteriology and virology, as to be almost useless. Manfred Eigen was forced to invent the term "quasi-species" to account for the speed of viral mutation,[8] and the term will almost certainly become more widely used to avoid false connotations. The conceptual branches on the tree, which Darwin took to be distinct species, are now found to be often related horizontally as well as vertically, as genes cross the species barrier in ways, at evolutionary periods, and with mechanisms that are extremely obscure. "It's part of a revolutionary change in biology .... Our standard model of evolution is under enormous pressure," says one commentator. More bluntly, says another, "The tree of life is being politely buried, we all know that [but] what's less accepted is that our whole fundamental view of biology needs to change."[9] In a word, biology is at a crossroads.

No doubt Darwin, were he alive today, would at first be bewildered by all these new developments, but there is no reason to think that he would have felt threatened by them, for he did not think of himself as having proprietary rights over the theory that bears his name. Darwin was that rare scientist, a superb observer and experimentalist and a philosopher, and these recent discoveries take evolutionary theory to a level where exceptional philosophical imagination and logical power are needed if progress is to be made. It is building up, if slowly. Nearly half a century ago C.H. Waddington suggested that we need a metabiology, but it was not until 1985 that the journal *Biology and Philosophy* appeared. In 1988 Ernst Mayr, raised awareness of biology's hidden dilemma in *Towards a New Philosophy of Biology*, for, as he said, biology could not help but be the "study of end-directed processes." How was this to be reconciled with non-purposive evolution? Colin Pittendrigh invented the term "teleonomy" to clothe the purposive factor in some respectable Darwinian garb and avoid the red rag term "teleology" that biology had inherited from Aristotle. The change of label did not, however, fool the arch-Darwinian Jacques Monod, who called it "a profoundly ambiguous concept," and later Richard Dawkins brought out his conceptual howitzer of the "selfish gene" to dispose of the ambiguity once and for all. But the problem has not gone away, and its resolution will set the agenda for a paradigm change in biology. This would have radical effects on the direction of research, but would not make much change at field or bench level. One waits for a new theorist, or metatheorist, with Darwin's ability to think big, with his imaginative power and, not least, with his scientific honesty.

References

1. Given that the sense of a higher reality (call it God) must have a locus in the brain, it is also possible that Darwin's religious faith was diminished by the debilitating and depressive illness which plagued him for many years, and which, it has been hypothesized, may have been contracted in the tropics as a young man. A neurosurgeon friend once told me of a patient on whom he had performed a lobotomy as a last resort to relieve extreme neuralgia. After the operation she reported to him that she had lost the pain, but also that she had lost all sense of God, which so distressed her that she said she would have preferred to live with the pain. The neurological and theological implications are significant.

2. Review in *New Scientist* (16. 8. 96)

3. Review in *Trends in Ecology and Evolution* (4. 4. 97)

4. Michael Denton, *Evolution: A Theory in Crisis*. London: Ebury Press, 1985.

5   cf. Michael Crawford and David Marsh, *The Driving Force: Food in Evolution and the Future*. London: Heinemann, 1989.

6. J. Cairns, J. Overbaugh, S. Miller, "The Origin of Mutants", *Nature* 335, 142 -5, 1988.

7. See, e.g., "Adaptive Mutation: the Debate Goes On", *Science 269, July 21, 1995*.

8. Manfred Eigen, *Steps Towards Life: Perspectives on Evolution*. OUP, 1996.

    Also as contributor to *Quasispecies and RNA Virus Evolution: Principles and Consequences*. Austin TX: Landes Bioscience, 2002.

9. Quotes from Graham Lawton, "Uprooting Darwin's Tree," *New Scientist*, 24 January 2009.

Part 3:

LOOKING FORWARD:

NEOTHEOLOGY

Theology was once called "the queen of sciences," and if that seems quaint today, it is worth remembering that the word "God" has always been used to label ultimate reality. That we, as near relatives of apes, do not have complete knowledge of ultimate reality should not surprise us.

In the West, the "science of God" developed through systematic theology, organised like other sciences with its own methods and axioms, and built upon its own taxonomy. This has varied from time to time, but conventionally includes such disciplines as scriptural, moral, pastoral, dogmatic, mystical theology and so on. This section of the book is put forward as a first cut at the ground plan for a new kind of systematic theology, incomplete but, hopefully, suggestive of hidden possibilities.

The titles of the section indicate areas where there is common cause with science. One critical omission is experimental theology, but there is reason to think that where cosmotheology and neurotheology come together fertile new ground for mystical awareness will be found.

HISTORICAL THEOLOGY AND TRUTH

The world is divided into so-called "faith groups," so that a map could be coloured to show vast areas, and whole continents, which are Christian (Catholic and Protestant), Moslem, Buddhist, Hindu, Confucian and animist. Despite all the fine ideals of mutual understanding, there is no likelihood that the barriers between them will ever be removed, since a religion defines one's natural community and is a tacit statement about what it means to be fully human. In the end, ecumenism can do little more than reach agreement to differ and to give equal status and value to all groups. This has some value in minimizing conflict, but leaves fundamental issues untouched. How does one, for instance, establish a relationship of mutual toleration with a group for whom religious toleration is a weakness, if not a moral defect? How does one accord equal values to a religion which offends one's sense of human dignity, as, for instance, in the way it treats women?

Several important conclusions can be drawn from this summary overview. Firstly, despite the relativistic climate of our time, it is clear that all religions are not of the same value, and we need a metatheology to establish what is higher or lower. Metatheology, it is worth noting, is a branch of metascience. Secondly, a direct appeal to members of any religion to look at it critically would be futile, for they will feel they are being invited to attack their self-identity. Thirdly, since every religion is a tacit definition of what is human nature – or, more accurately, human potential - we shall get nowhere in our quest for common understanding until we take positive steps to know why we have such different religious understandings. It will not just happen: we must work to know where every religion is coming from, and not least the one to which we give our loyalty.

The last conclusion is a Catch 22, because a religious truth is a truth as defined by a particular religion, and is protected from questioning, effectively tabooed. A wall of defensiveness is thrown up as soon as one seeks to analyze the very issues that define a religion. In this situation historical theology can be used as a Trojan horse to get through the psychological defences by looking first at how other religions than our own have evolved. In the West the most predominant religion today is probably agnosticism, sometimes referred to as couldn't-care-less-ism, so what follows is relevant only to those who feel a curiosity about religious matters.

Before going further, it needs to be agreed that religion as such is concerned with honesty in the face of evidence, for while science prides itself on this (not always with justification) there would be no consensus among religionists. In fact, it is probable that most religionists would rate intellectual honesty as far less desirable than tribal loyalty. One might, in fact, sum up their position in a paraphrase of the famous words about patriotism uttered by Stephen Decatur "My religion! May it be always right but, right or wrong, my religion." Total honesty is rarely within our reach, since, as the following essay on neurotheology will argue, it is often deformed by emotional or social factors. It is quite possible, for instance, for a mother to be completely convinced that the man who stands with a smoking gun over the corpse is innocent of the crime, if that man happens to be her son. In a similar way, it is possible for a religionist to believe that black is white if this is what his religious community demands of him.

With this proviso, that our individual and community conscience can sometimes be in conflict, I will suggest that seekers of religious truth can avoid the minefield of wired-in prejudice by approaching religion historically in two stages, first by looking at the history of a religion other than their own. Then, when they have come to take for granted that other religions have a historical origin, mutate in doctrine, and create myths, self-delusions and power structures, let them turn attention to their own religion. This is by no means a guarantee that their defensive reflex will not over-ride any unwelcome evidence, but it will at least sow a seed of suspicion that may bear fruit in the future. A little parable will help illustrate the benefits that may be expected from adopting historical awareness as a new perspective. It concerns two men, each of whom possessed a fine horse, and when their father died, they found that two thirds of his estate had been willed to the one whose horse finished last in a mile long race – not first, but last. On an appointed day they went off from the starting line, each trying any delaying tactic to make their horse lose, pulling on the reins, circling round, backtracking, but after an hour of this futility, both gave up. In despair at ever overcoming the problem, they consulted the wise old woman of the local village, and she solved it immediately in four words – "Mount each other's horse."

The way in which religions evolve makes for a fascinating study, and none moreso than the evolution of the Judaic and Christian religions. While an outsider can see that Judaism has a core of mythology in such things as the waters of the Red Sea parting to let the Israelites escape from Egypt, or Jahweh handing over his ten commandments to Moses on tablets of stone, pious Jews are able to live, almost like children, in a hazy, ambiguous world where myth and history do not have clear outlines. It is only in the past century and a half that scholars have seriously attempted to find the historical basis of the pattern of myth on which Judaism is based, and what they have discovered is a story that touches the old mythology in some places, but in others functions almost as a competing mythology. We can be sure, for instance, that Moses was an Egyptian (as his name would indicate – cf. Tutmoses) and a proponent of the religion of the reforming Pharaoh Ahkenaton. The facts emerge from archaeology and linguistics, beginning as speculations, then strengthening into hypotheses, and eventually hardening into accepted historical fact; but however convincing the evidence may be to an outsider, it rarely has any power to convince those who live by the traditional mythology. One Jew who had the courage to confront the historical evidence was Sigmund Freud, who concluded without qualification that "Moses was not a Jew but an Egyptian,"[1] but he outraged his fellow Jews, almost without exception, for saying so. Few wished to know whether or not it was true.

At the centre of all religions is a concept of "god" – a word one should perhaps always put in quotation marks – and historical scholarship is now revealing that beneath Jewish monotheism is a fascinating fusion of three gods. The sole divinity of Akhenaton, which he had identified with the sun as giver of life on earth, had been rejected by the Egyptians, for the conservative priestly establishment, whose professional authority was inseparably tied to a polytheistic religion of ancient half-animal divinities which abound in representations going back four thousand years. Horus, the falcon god, Anubis, the jackal god, Thoth the ibis god, etc. are ubiquitous. It has long been known that the Egyptians rejected Akhenaton's new theological perception, and obliterated its traces in a wave of iconoclasm, but only for a century or so has it been realised that it was taken up by the Hebrews under Egyptian leadership and carried with them in their exodus. It is hardly too fanciful to see a historical parallel in the way that the Mormons went west to Utah with Brigham Young in the nineteenth century, for exodus is a typical pattern of action when a new religion cannot coexist with the old. From this perspective Judaism began as an Egyptian heresy, but the story takes many twists thereafter (since theology was a very fluid thing at the time) and eventually the "new" god of the Hebrews, which appears in the Old Testament as Adonai (from the "-aton" root), merged with the great Semitic divinity El, which is still to be found in Al-lah and Isra-el, and with the Hebrews' tribal divinity Jahweh, who was initially a secondary god who caused storms, thunders and volcanoes.

From this thumbnail history two things are worth singling out in the present context. Firstly, the myth functioned as a vehicle for a high ethical code, and Jews were so aware of the uniqueness of their religion in this regards that they dismissed all non-Jews as "sinners" and routinely referred to them as pigs and dogs.[2] We take for granted that religion is concerned with morality, but that was not the case until the Jews discovered, or invented, a God who was not only powerful but "holy". There is no evidence of contemporary religions having a god that was interested in ethical behaviour, let alone one who codified it on a tablet of stone and made it the centre of his cult. The Law, which Jews still regard as their greatest treasure and gift from God, was in effect, *and was intended to be,* a specification for the complete human being – the righteous man. The second thing to be singled out from the primitive religion of the Jews is the way in which theology was twisted in order to justify the invasion and settlement of the territory occupied by the Canaanites and other tribes. Their god "told them to do it", ostensibly because the land he wanted them to occupy was a "wilderness of sin." Land clearance does not come more genocidal than the detailed instructions recorded in the books of *Joshua* and *Deuteronomy*, where Jahweh gives his instructions: "In the cities of these nations whose land the Lord your God is giving you as a patrimony, you shall not leave any creature alive, you shall eliminate them" (Deuteronomy 20:16ff.).

This inhuman god has bothered many Christian commentators, not least John Calvin, who managed to his satisfaction to reconcile it with the same divinity that Jesus preached as a god of love. It does not, however, seem to bother Jews so much as the historians' conclusion that Judaism was founded by an Egyptian, which is simply taken to be unbelievable. The baneful effects of the myth that God commanded the Hebrews to exterminate the original inhabitants of Palestine are felt still today. It provided moral justification for the Irgun terrorists during the late period of the British mandate of Palestine, and then for the expulsion of Arabs from a re-founded Israel. However, my main purpose here is to reveal a largely hidden link between what might be called the Joshua myth and the Christian myth.

The Christian myth is a mirror image of the Jewish in two interesting ways. Firstly, the Christian god is a fusion of two tribal divinities, just as the Jewish god was a fusion of three, and historical scholarship reveals that the founder of Christianity was not what the myth says he was, just as Moses was not a Hebrew. The thrust of the gospels is to show that Jesus was a kind of post-Jew or honorary gentile, and John's gospel even reports him telling his fellow Jews that they are the spawn of Satan (8:44). What dreadful persecution of the Jews this historical lie has justified over the centuries is immeasurable, but since it is taken to be "gospel truth," there is no official reason to question its historical truth. The story is part of a concerted attempt by the evangelists to rewrite history, in order to establish that Jesus came to found a new religion, which would be post-Jewish and thus incipiently anti-Jewish. Evidence for this crops up everywhere, once one is alerted to the hypothesis, but is difficult to collate, because the main source is the gospels, and they were written at least a generation after the events, we do not know who wrote them and they clearly have been drastically edited by unknown hands. How much does one know about the real Jesus without this kind of background information? Probably as much as one would know about Orwell's *Animal Farm* if one did not know of its unstated political agenda. Without awareness that the book was written as an attack on totalitarianism, we must read it simply as an animal fable.

There is, of course, a scholarly industry in scriptural analysis, but to take one typical problem, Luke's gospel recounts how Jesus on the cross prayed, "Father forgive them, for they know not what they do," (Luke 23:24) but the very earliest manuscript we possess does not contain that verse, and there may well be an earlier one still, now lost, which did contain it. Was it added by some pious copyist, as the sort of thing Jesus would have said, or was it missed by accident, or deliberately omitted? Given that Jesus is the model of a forgiving person, one might be inclined to think it could not possibly have been taken out on purpose, but the antagonism between Jews and Christians that had arisen by the time that Luke was writing does not make that a secure theory by any means, for passions were running high. It is perfectly possible that these inspiring words were not there in the original, but were added, then possibly deleted by one copyist who felt it was going too far to forgive those who had killed a god-man. On the fiftieth anniversary of Auschwitz, Elie Wiesel, who had received the Nobel prize for "spiritual leadership" and founded The Elie Wiesel Foundation for Humanity, prayed on the site, "God of forgiveness, do not forgive ... God of mercy, have no mercy on those who killed here Jewish children." The twist to the story of Jesus is that he is supposed by Christians to have been forgiving his fellow Jews, as he hung on the cross, but it was the Romans who crucified him, and forgiving them would have created in him a real crisis of conscience, since God clearly wanted them out of the land he had given to his chosen people.

Although the gospels attempt to portray Jesus as, at the least, a non-tribal Jew with global vision and a mission to save all humans, his own words, as recorded in the gospel of Matthew give the lie to this invention. Not only did he declare that his mission was to "the lost sheep of the house of Israel and to no one else" (Matthew 15:24) but he even forbade his message to be given to non-Jews, (Matthew: 10:5). As a committed Jew, he would have regarded a holy land polluted by Roman occupiers as a permanent affront to the divine will and, like other Jews, would have particularly hated the tax farmers, the "publicans" of the gospels. In the context of his Jewish exclusiveness, it simply makes no sense to hear of him sitting down and eating with tax-gatherers and sinners (Mark 2:16), since, as just noted, "sinners" was the deprecatory term applied by Jews to all non-Jews. Eating together was, so to speak, kinship in action, and it is noteworthy in this context how Paul was forbidden by headquarters in Jerusalem (and specifically by James the brother of Jesus) to let his Christian converts in Antioch mix with gentile converts at meal time (Galatians 2:12). There was clearly great confusion at that time about what constituted a Christian identity. When one knows the political background, it is jaw-dropping to read of Jesus telling everyone to pay their taxes like good Roman citizens (cf. Mark 12:16), far less likely than General de Gaulle telling his fellow Frenchmen to cheerfully accept the German occupation of his country. When Jesus tells his followers to sell their cloaks in order to buy swords (Luke 22:36), the obvious question must be asked, against whom did he want the swords to be used? The only answer can be "the Roman invaders," for Jewish spirituality was inseparable from Jewish independence – it was the will of God.

Under the tangled evidence, the key to understanding why Christianity developed in the way it did must be that Paul came to recognize something uniquely spiritual about the man Jesus, the same quality that inspired his Jewish followers. This he expressed in various letters and various ways, but most strikingly in "the revelation of the glory of God in the face of Jesus Christ" (2 Cor 4:6), an intriguing phrase, since he had never met Jesus, so far as we know. After the experience of his own revelation, it would seem, he felt an overwhelming call to propagate the message of God-in-man by packaging it in a form that the Graeco-Roman world could understand. What we know today as the Jesus of faith is an amalgam of Jewish prophet and the Apollo of Greek mythology, the ideal human who was the son of the great god Zeus. It would seem that this possibility came to Paul literally in a blinding stroke on the road to Damascus. Its religious dynamic is proved by the fact it seeded a new civilization, but religion must now move on, for we live in a post-Pauline world.

The problem that faces us, and leaves us at a crossroads of indecision, is the difficulty of going beyond the myth, which now has a life of its own, and is part of history. It may be dying, but is far from dead and may be compared to an old and decaying tree which has boughs that still produce sweet fruit. As the evidence mounts that Jesus was a Jew, and never intended to found a church, a feeling of disorientation must come over anyone who has been brought up to believe that he was the only Son of God, the Prince of Peace and the Saviour of the World. Unravelling the historical falsehoods which have become integral to Christian belief is a long and discouraging task, for all the forensic work must seem at first to be completely negative in its effect, seeming only to destroy "faith" without putting anything better in its place and leaving the simple believer bewildered and adrift. This is why dedication to truth in religion may seem at first as a kind of anti-gospel, and will generate the same feelings of fear and anger that the original Jewish followers of Jesus must have experienced when they encountered Paul's "gospel to the gentiles." For these reasons, a passion for historical truth, however strongly felt, must be tempered with concern for those of good intent who cannot take it neat, and that is probably applicable to most of us. So many factors must be weighed before making a decision to go for historical truth, that it might be compared to the surgeon's hesitation in facing a patient with a tumour near the brain. Simply to excise it may not be the answer, for that could kill or disable the patient, exactly the opposite of what is required. Decisiveness is called for, but caution too, and no small measure of love and wisdom. Patience would seem to be the counsel of Jesus himself, since among his sayings is the advice to leave wheat and weeds to grow up together until the time is appropriate, "lest the wheat be pulled up with the weeds." However, with our current knowledge of the gospels, we must question why he said this, or if he said it.

The overarching theme of this essay is that the world is at a religious crossroads, unable to go further because each of the great faith groups is locked into a self-reinforcing mythology, assumed by its members to be both permanent and self-evidently superior. No way has yet been found to change this situation, and so the religious evolution of the human race is at a standstill. I have argued that an essential factor in making progress must be a historical study of religion. There is nothing particularly new about that, and it is certainly not proposed here as some sort of universal remedy. It may be necessary, but is certainly not sufficient. My approach is unusual in assuming that in our time curiosity is as essential an element in spiritual development as it is in science. In the longer view, it may be an intellectual scaffolding whose usefulness ends when the non-intellectual part of religious experience has developed – that is, the wordless awe, the gratitude, the sense of presence. The point and purpose of religion is, after all, to go beyond the rational: as Eckhart put it, there is nothing in creation so like God as stillness. In different degrees, however, curiosity is an essential scaffolding for all. Those who support blind obedience in matters of religion are aborting the evolutionary process, whether they realise it or not.

My approach is also unusual, and seemingly negative, in assuming that few in any religion will be curious to know about other religions, and very few will wish to examine their own religion with the same kind of informed and impartial judgement that they are happy to bring to others. For these few who feel a need to know – and they are probably five per cent or less – the rewards will be ambiguous. They will certainly receive no encouragement from within their own group; doubt and uncertainty will be their chosen lot for a long time, perhaps for many years, and they will be lucky if they encounter like-minded seekers to give mutual support. Even when one is prepared for "the shock of the new" in relation to one's familiar belief system, it would be advisable to make progress slowly. One cannot underestimate the psychological resistance to rejecting familiar beliefs, which are not so much single propositions as mutually reinforcing parts of a psychological structure. With this in mind, one might think of Gulliver, tied down by a thousand threads, and able to escape only if these are severed patiently one by one.

With this principle in mind, I have given below, in the References,[3] the titles of some books on the nature of history and on Judaeo-Christianity which may be helpful in severing the threads, so to speak, starting with those which are a more gentle initiation into an unfamiliar way of thinking about religion. I have not included books on other religions, but only because that would weaken the cohesion of my theme, which, heaven knows, is wide enough. Scores of popular books on the historical Jesus have become available in the last twenty years, representing various perspectives, biases and often clear prejudices. The more one reads, the more an outline of common perception appears despite the differences. I must emphasize that the samples I provide are half a dozen out of perhaps fifty that could have been listed, and many excellent works have been omitted, but they will enable the curious to make a start.

References

1. Sigmund Freud, *Moses and Monotheism*, trans. Katherine Jones. New York: Vintage Books, 1967 (1939). p.

2. Without this historical awareness we miss something of impor-
    tance when reading about Jesus commanding that the pearls of
    his wisdom should not be given to swine (Matthew 7:6) or talk-
    ing about giving food to dogs, when he hesitated before healing
    the gentile Syro-Phoenician woman (Mark 7:26). We have so
    universalized and divinized Jesus that discovering he had Jewish
    reflexes can have an almost traumatic effect.

3. There is still no better introduction to historical and comparative
    religion than William James's 1901 Gifford Lectures on Natural
    Religion, published and reprinted many times as *The Varieties
    of Religious Experience*. I am far from alone in finding in it fresh
    insight fifty years after my first reading. In fact, I think one may
    need experience to appreciate how exceptional a work it is.

An excellent introduction to metahistory, illustrating the pitfalls
to be avoided in reading any history, are explored in E. H. Carr's
best-selling and very short *What is History?* (1961). Although Carr
has serious shortcomings as a historian, his advice to "listen for
the bee in the historian's bonnet" is crucial in reading religious
history.

Popular histories of Judaism tend towards quite different align-
ments, depending on whether they are written "from the inside"
by Jews or "from the outside" by gentiles. The worst traps in each
case are avoided in Norman Cantor's *The Sacred Chain* (1995),
which offended many Jews and Christians in describing the Old
Testament as "romantic fantasy," and Paul Johnson's *A History
of the Jews* (1988), which is both readable and sympathetic. In
neither, however, is the significance of a mythic Abraham and
an Egyptian Moses brought out fully. The full extent of the Old
Testament borrowings from Egyptian myth and history is covered
in Gary Greenberg's *101 Myths of the Bible: How Ancient Scribes
Invented Biblical History* (2000). Greenberg is president of the
Biblical Archaeology Society of New York, and this account of
religious myth-building is comprehensive and scholarly, but at
the same time readable. It is, however, more perhaps for reference
and dipping in than straight-through reading.

Of histories of Jesus and Christianity there is no end, or at least
it seems so, and the best are often swallowed up in a tide of the
mediocre. The following are graded more or less in order of shock
effect. In fact, for someone coming new to this field there is a
genuine benefit in starting with the less up-to-date works, for

this allows time for what once seemed too unorthodox for belief to become a familiar part of one's intellectual landscape.

Albert Nolan's, *Jesus Before Christianity* (1977, but now in its fifteenth reprinting) is by a South African Catholic priest, and an honest mix between open-mindedness and conservative assumptions.

Russell Shorto's *Gospel Truth* (1997), by a well-informed American journalist, covers more ground at more depth, and raises more questions

Donald Akenson, *Saint Saul: A Skeleton Key to the Historical Jesus* (2000), by a Canadian historian, is more scholarly, but very readable, and drives relentlessly to the point that many Christians refuse to accept, and indeed find incredible, that Christianity was a religion founded by Paul. From this perspective, Jesus was an exceptional, spiritually evolved human, but Paul was a theological innovator, a religious genius and, it must be said, a consummate spin doctor, a blusterer, and a very brave man. Without his insight and persistence Jesus of Nazareth would be no more a hinge of history than Honi, the Circle Drawer – a point made by Geza Vermes in *Jesus the Jew* (1973). Vermes, born a Jew, converted to Christianity when he was seven, and later studied for the Catholic priesthood, but then reverted to Judaism, and has spent a long scholarly career in effect explaining why.

Barrie Wilson, *How Jesus Became Christ* (2008). By a Canadian cultural philosopher, looks at much the same facts as the authors above, and reaches a similar conclusion.

When all the scholarly work is over, and a consensus of agreement reached, the big question still remains: what religious action can or should be taken to accommodate the new historical truth?

COSMOTHEOLOGY AND CREATION*

In *Where is Science Going?* (1932) Max Planck wrote:

> *Science cannot solve the ultimate mystery of nature. And that is because, in the last analysis, we ourselves are part of the mystery that we are trying to solve.*

What he saw as a limitation to science can be viewed positively, however, as a theological revelation, for the discovery that our familiar universe had an origin in time ultimately leads to awareness that the creating power is at one with all that is created - everything is within it and it is within everything.

This, I would take it, is the intuition of Jesus and of countless other mystics in all the world's religions, but it is a truth which traditional religion has failed to teach and develop, even though a feeling of one-ness with a greater power is by no means uncommon among quite ordinary people. In his classic 1900 work *Cosmic Consciousness* the psychiatrist Richard Bucke gave many instances of this, and there are thousands of accounts of this kind of unitary eperience in the Archives of the Religious Experience Research Centre at the University of Wales in Lampeter. A well known passage from Admiral Byrd's autobiographical work *Alone* (1938) may speak for all, and illustrate their commonality. He tells of going outside one evening during his spell in Antarctica, as the sun was setting, and of his experience

> *"of the imponderable processes and forces of the cosmos, harmonious and soundless .... In that instant I could feel no doubt of man's oneness with the universe. The conviction came that that rhythm was too orderly, too harmonious, too perfect to be a product of blind chance - that, therefore, there must be purpose in the whole and that man was a part of the whole and not an accidental off-shoot, [that] the universe was a cosmos, not a chaos; man was as rightfully a part of that cosmos as were the day and night."* [1]

I would like to make three points regarding this spiritual experience and its connection with religion and a theology based on post-Hubble cosmology:

---

*Revised version of talk originally given to CANA (Christians Awakening to a New Awareness) at Birmingham University, Dec. 8, 2006.

- it is a perfect example of what the psychologist Abraham Maslow calls a "peak experience", and not necessarily connected with any religious belief
- religion should aim not to induce such peak experiences, but to generate an habitual awareness of oneness at a lower level of intensity
- modern cosmology offers invaluable help in generating this sense of spiritual oneness

The systematic use of cosmological science to help develop spiritual awareness would constitute an evolutionary step in religion, and hence a new term is called for to mark its significance. "Cosmotheology" springs naturally to mind, although the word already exists in a less specific sense than I wish to propose.[2] I would like to give a sharp definition of cosmology based on three clear postulates, as follows:

i. that hyperspace is real in more than just a mathematical sense
ii. that the expanding cosmos can be most effectively modelled as a thermodynamic system
iii. that a scientific cosmogony (i.e., theory of the origin of the universe) is a creation story with religious significance

From this position I will argue that cosmotheology presents us with a creative resolution of the historical conflict between the transcendental and immanentist models of God – that is to say, theologies of God without and God within. In the precise sense that I will use the term, cosmotheology promises to show how such theologies which are apparently exclusive are, in fact, mutually supportive and mutually illuminating.

The great revolution in cosmology that began with discovery of the galactic redshift is our awareness that we live in an expanding universe. Its vital importance to theology lies in the reasonable assumption that the more cosmology reveals about the processes of creation, the more it will reveal about the nature of the creating power. From this perspective, it marks a significant advance in the evolution of religion, for it is based solidly on empirical observation. Thus it is a prime example of the kind of fact-based theology which the late Arthur Peacocke argued must become a new standard for religion. Religion, he says, must "become truly open theologically" and theologians need "frankly to infer the best explanation of the data - and not build theological castles in the air based on historically unsupported events ... and on outdated metaphysical systems."[3]

To his argument I would add that this is the first time in history that intellectual honesty, which is an essential in science, must now become a defining criterion of authentic or evolved religion. This being accepted, although cosmology is still piecing together the creation story, it becomes not one option among many but, in making all other creation myths obsolescent, it becomes a theological imperative. Thus cosmotheology will ultimately become a moral imperative, for it is wrong to tell stories as factual that we know to be untrue. It is not even necessary to retain the old creation fables for children, since the story that science is telling is as simple, as entertaining and, dare one say, as romantic as anything in the Bible, the Koran or the Vedas.

The theology which follows from the new cosmology will be paradigmatic in several respects, not least in being dynamic. By "dynamic" I mean that it inherently defines religion as a transforming way of life involving a new sense of human identity. It leads not just to passive acceptance of great theological truths, such as Tillich's definition of God as "the ground of being," but to a deeper kind of awareness, where these truths are, in Wordsworth's words, "felt in the blood, and felt along the heart." It leads, in a word, to a more intimate relationship between the human and divine, indeed to a blurring of the "I and Thou" relationship which Martin Buber proposed as an ideal. More controversially perhaps - but we must at all cost be honest - it will go beyond the "loving father" metaphor that is central to the teaching of Jesus, and the trinitarian model of divinity which gave birth to Western civilisation. In the long term view it is potentially a new model for a global civilisation. In this respect, cosmotheology raises the religious bar, as ethical monotheism and trinitarianism raised it in the past.

Like all paradigmatic shifts in religion, closer identification of the divine and human, to which cosmotheology leads, will be on first encounter a shock. It will come as either a new good news or an affront to orthodoxy, live-giving or life-threatening, an inspiring truth suddenly recognized or an alien idea to be rejected. Despite its unfamiliarity, which may make it appear at first like heresy, its practical conclusions are, in fact, a natural extension of the God-in-man theologies which are common to Judaeo-Christianity, Islamic Sufism and Vedic Hinduism but have never become mainstream. Insfar as man creates God in his own image, there is much here to be clarified, but no reason to prevent a clarification.

A simple thought experiment will reveal the significance of a theology based on cosmic evolution. If we wind back in imagination the film of cosmic expansion, we come to the realisation that all that now exists, including each individual consciousness, must have its origin in the energetic reality that can be traced back to the singularity of the Big Bang. If the expanding cosmos is taken to be a closed system (as a working assumption at this stage), everything within it now must have been there in potential at every earlier stage, much as an oak tree may be said to have been contained *in potentia* in an acorn.[4] Judaeo-Christianity has missed this truth, because it has traditionally emphasized the doctrine of creation from nothing. Cosmotheology, by contrast, throws it into stark relief and disposes once and for all of the illusion that there once was a sky god working magic on a nothing to make it into a something. The reality is, as the poet put it, that

> The lark, the shark, the cloud, the clod,
> The whole darned universe is God" [5],

But human consciousness is God in a very special and challenging way.

As this conclusion starts to come home, religion will enter into a new axial age, going from monotheism to panentheism and beyond that to a new awareness, which I call entheism, to indicate a deeply experiential and cooperative form of spirituality. We can see now, as past ages could not, that human beings are in a quite astonishing way agents in the evolutionary drama. We are the only species that can evolve deliberately, and thus the future of the species, and of the planet, is in our hands. We have reached a stage in our evolution where we can consciously accept that we are in the most literal sense co-creators or, by contrast, we can reject this possibility. The decision is ultimately our own, but the sort of encouragement we receive from the religious community will play a large part in the choice we make.

References

1. Richard E. Byrd, *Alone*. 1938. Various editions still in print.
2. "Cosmotheology" was, for instance, the title and theme of a Templeton conference held in 1998 to discuss the effects upon theology of modern cosmology, but used there very loosely, to cover "a diverse collection of musings", as one reviewer put it, mostly concerning possible life and religion on other planets. The proceedings can be found in Steven J. Dick (ed.), *Many Worlds: the New Universe, Extraterrestrial Life, and the Theological Implications*. Templeton Foundation Press, 2000.

3. 'Problems in Contemporary Christian Theology,' *Theology and Science, 2 (1),* (2004) p.3.

4. The analogy is oversimple, since to go from acorn to oak tree requires energetic input from outside the acorn itself, in the form of water, minerals and sunlight. Neither oak nor acorn is a closed system, and the question of whether or not our cosmos is a closed system is theologically critical and will be critical in defining neoscience.

5. From a short poem of Robert Service, entitled simply "God".

NEUROTHEOLOGY AND FREE WILL

"I am the master of my fate,
I am the captain of my soul."

W. E. Henley, *Invictus*, 1887

Many people have found Henley's well known lines inspirational, but their truth has come under increasing scrutiny by psychological and neurological studies, not least Benjamin Libet's evidence that our brain makes a decision several milliseconds before we are conscious of making it.[1] This leads to Sean Spence's conclusion that

> "if the notion of free will is to be retained by philosophers, psychiatrists and psychologists, it will be a free will which is essentially non-conscious."[2]

A non-conscious free will may seem to be a contradiction in terms, but is compatible with the position I have reached, through the different paths of psychosociology and history. My conclusion is that whatever else may be said about the freedom of the will as a unitary entity it is related to a shifting balance between different kinds of will. Some of these have identifiable centres within the brain but others arise from social relationships.

The existence in the individual of more than one will has long been recognized by psychologists in various disorders, among them obsessive-compulsive behaviour, Tourettism, auditory hallucinations (hearing voices which give orders and advice) and the so-called "alien hand" syndrome. The latter offers particularly dramatic evidence that two wills can co-exist within the individual, since a patient with this disorder will find one hand performing an action independently of his or her conscious will and seek to restrain it with the other hand. The action could be simply unbuttoning a jacket, but is often more embarrassing. The alien hand seems to have a life of its own, because it has a will of its own, a will that is in opposition to what I recognize as <u>my</u> will. That is to say, despite there being different centres of will in the brain, there seems to be one which defines the <u>real me</u>. An act of will has the power to trigger physical movement, but even the finest of hair triggers is an energetic system in itself, and both the biological and theological problem of free will could be expressed in the question, whose finger is on the trigger?

There is also a poorly researched area of social psychology dealing with the way in which my individual consciousness relates to cultural consciousness and can sometimes be in conflict with it. Evolutionary progress in the human species can only come about, in fact, when these two types of consciousness – individual and communal - are in temporary imbalance. In such a situation the individual, or a small group, feels unable to accept certain principles or beliefs which society at large takes for granted. Examples may be the morality of slavery or belief in a sun-centred universe. Cultural consciousness may be of a political, religious or scientific nature, but in all cases going against the assumptions and values of the group in serious matters generates a state of stress within the individual, which may be disturbing in either a creative or destructive way - Hans Selye's eustress and distress.

The important point here is that what I consider to be "my will" is very often really the will of the community acting through my brain. Were I to have been accidentally switched at birth in hospital (as happens) and given to a devout Moslem or Jewish family, I would grow up wired with unquestionable religious assumptions which I would consider to be my own. The question of community consciousness, and community will, is now entering into a critical evolutionary phase, as thinking people become aware of belonging to a global human family as well as to a particular national or religious group. Thus a new sense of self-identity is starting to emerge and with it a new centre of free will. There is no sense of a global religion emerging – indeed, the term sounds almost unhealthy - but there is widespread acceptance today of the logic that insists there cannot be a multiplicity of gods to validate all the world's conflicting religions.

Auditory hallucinations are of particular religious importance, since the whole of western history has been shaped by individuals who have "heard voices" and done what those voices have told them to do, often against their own expressed wishes. Examples range through Moses and the Hebrew prophets, Socrates, Mohamed and Augustine to Joan of Arc, George Fox and Swedenborg, as well as mystics in all religious traditions who have heard voices and seen visions. This kind of shamanic consciousness is also to be found in musicians and poets who feel that their inspiration was given to them in some sense from the outside, often from above. Mozart said that he received the complete form of a concerto or symphony in his head before he had put a note on paper. Similarly, one may quote from writers such as George Matheson, the composer of the well known hymn, "O Love that will not let me go." Of its composition he said, "I had the impression of having it dictated to me by some inward voice.... All the other verses I have ever written are manufactured articles: this came like a dayspring from on high." Shamanic these voices may be in a broad sense, but they are far from the passive seizures of primitive animism. In the Western tradition, prophesy goes along with a clear sense of self and a higher will in cooperation.

The sense of being inspired from "outside" one's normal consciousness is more rare in philosophy or science, but is by no means absent. Socrates acknowledged the debt he owed to his *daemon*, and, to take one example of many from science, Julius Mayer considered that the first law of thermodynamics (that energy can neither be created nor destroyed, but only transformed) was given to him as a religious insight, a revelation in the strictest sense.

While artistic inspiration of this kind is regarded as healthy and beneficial, with the rise of psychiatry spiritual inspiration through voices has become simply suspect and is classified as "auditory hallucination" whether their message is inspirational or completely delusional. As some wit remarked, when I talk to God, that is prayer, but when he talks to me, it is paranoid schizophrenia. Interestingly the great spiritual teachers have usually been as sceptical of raptures, visions and extreme emotional states as hard-nosed scientists. In *The Interior Castle* Teresa of Avila says that seeking such experiences should be treated like an illness (*"como enferma"*). William James, in *The Varieties of Religious Experience*, is ambiguous, acknowledging the public value of some "spiritual" revelations, but he describes the founder of the Quakers George Fox, for instance, as "a psychopath of the deepest dye," even though he regarded Quakerism as "a religion which it is impossible to overpraise." [3]

We are on the edge here of a rich field where history, theology and neuropsychology meet, and my contribution will be to comment on five aspects of free will that I believe offer great promise for research and for personal development alike. I will say nothing about genetic determinism, which opens up a whole new dimension to the issue of free will, and calls for at least a whole book – if not a university degree course. The last two of my proposals will project the curve of neurological and social evolution into a hypothesized future.

The first suggestion is that since free will must always be predetermined to some degree by cultural conditioning, its strengthening in the species must involve escape from national or religious indoctrination. It follows then that education should be undertaken with this in mind. Two hundred years ago Thomas Jefferson insisted that authentic democracy was impossible without education, and it is surely the case that authentic religion in the twenty first century is equally impossible without education of a non-religious kind. Tribal indoctrination is no substitute for spiritual enlightenment.

The second suggestion is that understanding free will is critically dependent on a basic knowledge of evolutionary neurology. Millions of years of evolution have left us with three overlaid and competing brains, and thus three competing wills. Paul MacLean, who first pointed it out, called them our reptilian, mammalian and human brains.[4] Building on this insight, other researchers have constructed a four-brain model, with part of the prefrontal cortex acting as a control centre. From this perspective, the prefrontal lobe may be considered as the seat of free will, if free will is taken to be essentially the power to control our actions, thought and feelings. This theme has been developed by Jonathan Sacks and Elkhonon Goldberg in *The Executive Brain*.[5]

Understanding the brain as tripartite, with each part both cooperating with and competing against the others reinforces the conclusion that free will is not such a fixed factor in the individual's consciousness as usually assumed. Our higher brain struggles constantly against evolutionary regression, and in matters great and small we have all experienced a kind of hijacking of free will, or at least of a higher self, when passion of one sort or another has overcome logic, commonsense or moral principle. Often we excuse it, or explain it, by saying, "I couldn't help myself," thus implying that my true self is a function of the control centre in a way that it is not a function of, say, my sex drive. In passing, one might note that the fantasy Jesus, which tends to dominate popular Christianity, is assumed to have had total control of the complex and unruly human brain, despite the gospel accounts of his violence against the moneychangers in the Temple and near breakdown in Gethsemane.

The third aspect of free will whose importance I would emphasize is that it is inseparable from the question, "Who am I?", which is assuming ever greater importance in the modern age. The psycho-historian Julian Jaynes argued that the critical threshold when self-consciousness emerged from "group-think" was crossed some three thousand years ago.[6] Before that time the individual did not need to think: it was the tribe and its leader who did the thinking for him or her. The transition to the clearly self-aware individual (by no means completed globally) seems to have happened first in ancient Greece after a transitional period of perhaps three of four centuries. Jaynes' central point, was that in the early part of the transition a fragile, almost alien, sense of self-autonomy coexisted with a pervading tribal consciousness, and that in times of stress the individual's reaction would be to regress and create for himself an external authority in the form of a voice which told him what to do. One might ask what is the relationship between this pathology (to the modern mind) and the voices heard by prophets and mystics. The answer is by no means so cut and dried as might at first appear.

Jaynes provides convincing evidence that the crossover from proto-human to fully human was via a long period of literal schizophrenia, which only came to an end as the *corpus callosum*, the tissue connecting the left and right brain, thickened and created more powerful and stable coordination between them, and it is reasonable – surely inevitable – that the next evolutionary step must involve a comparable change in brain structure.

My fourth proposal is a prediction that this change must occur in the reticular formation, and must be attempted deliberately. If this is accepted, or even considered at this stage, it would involve re-educating one of the most ancient parts of the brain, and setting up new pathways between the hippocampus and the reticular formation. The hippocampus is that part of the brain most directly concerned with acquiring new knowledge. The reticular formation has several basic functions. It is closely related to the autonomic systems, and thus by definition is outside free will, and it has a universal survival function, for it triggers alertness and focuses consciousness in the context of danger. When it comes into action, the human animal has no free will: it is as though our attention was seized by the sound or smell or visual impression that signals danger. It is active in the mother who picks up the slightest sounds from her child sleeping in another room, sounds which would be inaudible, because unnoticed, by someone else. It could be called the organ of significance, and is perhaps the seat of intuition.

As the species has evolved, the reticular formation seems to have developed overlaid functions, widening its scope in alerting us to more than danger. Does humankind's survival in the gathering global crisis call for a further extension? Although I am not aware that this has been proved experimentally, it is reasonable to suppose that it is critically involved in the appreciation of beauty and, if so, that it must be highly developed in the artistic individual. A flower or a sunset, a colour or pattern, will seize attention quite independently of the artist's will and, so to speak, carry with it significance, but not to those who lack sensitivity. As Wordsworth wrote of Peter Bell, "A primrose by the river's brim / A yellow primrose was to him / And it was nothing more." What we might call spiritual sensitivity seems to be an extension of this faculty. There is a story told of Ignatius Loyola in his retirement, overheard in the garden as he shook his stick at a bed of flowers and told them to stop shouting. I have not been able to check the historicity of this delightful story of synaesthetic confusion, but it is not implausible. The spiritually developed individual, in the Western tradition at least, seems to pick up signals of what Augustine famously called *pulchritudo tam antiqua et tam nova* – a beauty ever old and ever new - but a beauty that he addressed as "thou."

Although the reticular formation is largely outside the control of free will, it can, paradoxically, be educated, just as musicians can become pitch-sensitive and the artist's eye more appreciative by constant training. The possibilities, and the dangers, of using biofeedback to control it are well known, but have not yet been fully explored by any means. This leads me to propose that practical theology should have a central component of training the reticular formation to appreciate the beauty of creation as an essential part of knowing, and sharing, the beauty of the creating power. It hardly needs to be said that this suggestion will not make sense to the secularist who does not believe there is such a creating power in the first place, or at least one that has any relevance to the human species. It may well be, however, that secularism, which is rapidly becoming a quasi-scientific ortho-doxy, is not so much positive atheism as a healthy refusal to accept a broken-backed theology from the past. Despite refinements, the God of Christianity, and more obviously of Islam, is inherited from the Bronze Age culture of early Judaism, whose idea of a creating power was of a protective but capricious and despotic potentate above the clouds. It is high time that theology finally shook off this primitive mindset, and there could surely be no better way to start than by putting love of natural beauty much closer to the centre of theology than it has ever been.

In conclusion, my fifth suggestion, which bears on free will and religion, is that the spiral path of evolution is returning us to the same kind of critical rearrangement between self and society which happened in the past. We need now to reconnect with the group in order to create a desired kind of self, but this time by building an "imagined community." The term was originally used by Benedict Anderson to describe the nation state, but has a much wider signifi-cance. Put simply, my point is that if an authentic religion is assumed to be, above all, a spiritual community, and if the mystic is accepted as the most spiritually evolved human, an authentic religion must at least have mystical consciousness at its core.

Mysticism, however, is an anomalous condition in which the indi-vidual's self-identity is inseparable from identification with a higher reality – variously called God, Brahman, Allah, etc. The mystic in-tuits the reality, and senses the presence, of this higher reality and infers from this experience the existence of a higher will. Mysticism implies, therefore, two centres of self and of will. In this context, says the Sufi scientist Ali Ansari, self-realisation involves a "cognitive shift" in which "something deep and basic has happened at a neurological level."[7]

References

1. Benjamin Libet, *Neurophysiology of Consciousness*. Birkhauser Verlag AG, 1993. See also: "Do We Have Free Will," in *The Volitional Brain: Towards a Neuroscience of Free Will*. Exeter: Imprint Academic, 2000.

2. Sean A. Spence and Chris D Frith, "Towards a Functional Anatomy of Volition". In *The Volitional Brain* (ref. 1 above) See also: Sean A Spence and Anthony S David, *Voices in the Brain: The Cognitive Neuropsychiatry of Auditory Verbal Hallucination*. London: Psychology Press Ltd., 2005. Later researchers have concluded that one can only talk validly of a "free won't".

3. William James, *The Varieties of Religious Experience*. London: Fontana, 1969 [1902], p. 30. James was, of course, an eminent psychologist, and the subtitle of his Gifford Lectures was "A Study in Human Nature." It should perhaps be noted that he uses the word "psychopath" with overtones of misfit, not criminal.

4. Paul MacLean, *The Triune Brain in Evolution*. Kluwer Academic, 1990.

5. Oliver Sacks and Elkhonon Goldberg, *The Executive Brain: Frontal Lobes and the Civilized Mind*. NY: Oxford University Press, 2004

6. Julian Jaynes, *The Origin of Consciousness in the Breakdown of the Bicameral Mind*. NY: Houghton Mifflin, 2000 [1976].

7. Ali Ansari, *Sufism and Beyond: Sufi Thought in the Light of Late 20th Century Science*. Ahmedabad: Mapin Publishing, 2000. Distributed in the UK by Antique Collectors Club, Woodbridge, and in the US by Grantha Publishing, Middletown, NJ.

CHEMOTHEOLOGY
AND THE SPIRITUAL CHALLENGE

"Don't speak to me, my serotonin levels have hit bottom,
my brain is awash in glucocorticoids, my blood vessels
are full of adrenaline, and if weren't for my endogenous
opiates, I'd have driven the car into a tree on the way home.
My dopamine levels need lifting. Pour me a Chardonnay" [1]

Introducing Chemotheology

Four centuries ago Francis Bacon gave valuable advice about inventing neologisms. Since they were unfamiliar, and thus potentially an
obstacle to communication, he said that they should only be used
when they were necessary to communicate a genuinely new concept
or principle, On that basis the addition of chemotheology to the vo-
cabulary of science and religion is debatable, but justifiable *prima
facie* on two grounds. Firstly, although it may in some instances
seem only to express the obvious in a technical way, it may equally
draw attention to matters whose obviousness has obscured their
significance. To take one quick example, is the pleasure that the
worshipper, or meditator, obtains from the smell of incense spiritual
in any meaningful sense? What makes a smell spiritual or otherwise?
Chemotheology approaches these as important and open questions.
The second justification for introducing a new and unfamiliar term
is related to the first, but is more fundamental. Dealing as it does
with the physiological origins of all kinds of feelings, it offers help
in identifying genuine spirituality in a post-modern society that re-
sembles a spiritual bazaar, with no shortage of hucksters selling their
different nostrums.

Spirituality and Religion

It would be of value to begin with a working definition of the terms
"spirituality" and "religion", which are always in danger of being
confused. What follows assumes that spirituality is essentially a state
of consciousness marked by awareness of a higher reality with which
the individual feels, or desires to feel, a relationship. The term "God"
may be used as shorthand for this higher reality, though it carries
risk of misunderstanding because of its historical associations. Not

all in this secular age will feel that spirituality necessarily entails the sense of a higher reality, and Buddhists regard belief in a God, however defined, as an attachment that must be discarded if one is to experience reality. It is, nevertheless, the assumption of this paper that authentic spirituality involves a relationship, with practical consequences, between self-awareness and other-awareness.

Religion, by contrast with spirituality, is a corporate phenomenon, essentially a group composed of those who accept certain fundamental assumptions and agree not to question them. From a social scientist's point of view, therefore, a religion is a taboo system, unable to survive free enquiry about its constitutional beliefs from within its membership. It is worth noting, however, that science itself can become a taboo system, when questioning of fundamentals is forbidden. There is, in fact, a strong psychological connection between religious fundamentalism and scientism, both depreciating the individual's freedom to seek in favour of group-think.

Spirituality is a more general concept than religion, and it is often argued that there is a common factor of spirituality underlying all the world's different faith groups. This cannot be taken for granted, however, for a belief system and religious mythology are far more than a vehicle for spiritual awareness, and play a critical part in forming that awareness. Though the question is of vital importance in a world that seems to be entering into a "clash of civilizations," it will not be pursued here.

The New Theology

Chemotheology may be considered a branch of neurotheology, especially where it deals with neurotransmitters and neurosecretions, but has its own independence insofar as it focuses attention equally on the glandular system of the body, especially the endocrine system, where many of the chemicals that influence consciousness originate, Whether viewed as a free-standing discipline or not, it takes it place within a new kind of systematic theology that is now emerging in our scientific culture. Onto this all the traditional sub-categories – pastoral theology, dogmatic theology, etc – will eventually be mapped.

Cosmotheology, neurotheology and historical theology are together reshaping the theological landscape, and redefining religion, thus:

- *Cosmology is providing a new creation story which transcends the conflicting myths that keep the world in religious compartments and generate religious wars.*

- *Neurotheology is on the way to dissolving the barrier between a God "out there" and "God within."*
- *Historical theology is laying bare the pious fictions that have been taken for centuries as religious facts.*

Within this context, chemotheology offers a potential bridge between science and religion in an age where the need for such a bridge is increasingly felt and at the same time is a corrective to those who would argue that spirituality is only a higher kind of superstition. However, one must be realistic and recognize that since chemotheology spans both religion and science, it is more likely to be attacked from both sides than welcomed by either.

Naming the Parts

Like any science, chemotheology must start with a taxonomy. This paper will propose that the most significant classification on which to build is a set of those substances which play a role in altering moods and maintaining them. "Moods" is a rubbery term, and useful for that very reason, embracing diverse feelings such as happiness, anxiety, irritation, alertness and desire, which may be considered initially as an affective or emotional substrate against which thoughts and decision-making take place. A list of mind-altering chemicals can be organised in several ways, one natural division being between those which are produced by the body, those which occur in nature and those which are manmade. A further division can be made to distinguish between those substances whose effect is deliberately sought and those which generate changes of consciousness as a side effect. Another distinction could be between those which produce short-term and long-term changes in consciousness, and so on.

The link with theology arises most obviously from the possibility that some chemicals may generate, or assist in generating, spiritual awareness or, by contrast, may act to inhibit it. The questions that flow from this are of profound importance, and lead ultimately to the overarching question, what exactly is spiritual awareness? The simple taxonomy here proposed is no more than an indication of possible research programmes into the complex inter-connection between the body's neurochemicals and spiritual states, but it is a start. In the distant future one might envisage a three dimensional structure, creating a taxonomic space, but while this is an exciting philosophical prospect, it is far beyond the scope of this brief introduction.

With these considerations as background, the main chemicals produced by the body which act positively on our moods can be identified, though the need for important subclasses will soon appear, as will the need to trace their glandular origins and neurological pathways. The following list is the most general of overviews:

- *Adrenaline has a variety of effects, including giving one confidence and alertness, and is an effect of exercise, laughter, sexual or musical pleasure, among other things.*
- *Endorphins are released into the blood stream and the brain, usually when the adrenaline level reaches a critical point, and produce feelings of contentment.*
- *Serotonin makes one relaxed, tolerant and optimistic, and is produced by the action of sunlight, among other things.*
- *Cortisol controls stress levels and anxiety and works in tandem with adrenaline to keep the brain in dynamic balance, as well as having physical effects such as reducing inflammation.*
- *Melatonin is produced by darkness and is a relaxant which is necessary to send us to sleep.*
- *Insulin controls blood sugar levels, keeping a balance between the extremes of manic energy and lethargy.*

The relationship between the effects of these drugs is more complex than this list might suggest, but the important point is that any state of consciousness is always associated with one or more of them acting independently or in coordination and in different concentrations in the blood stream and the brain. More complex still is the question of the cause-effect relationship between mood and the production of chemicals, which is often of the chicken-and-egg variety. The stress of exercise, for instance, gives the benefits of adrenaline, but excessive adrenaline can amplify feelings of stress and create various undesirable changes in bodily functions and even changes in tissue. Before that state is reached, endorphins, which are natural opiates, are released to block the pain receptors in the nervous system. There is not, in general, a strict cause-and-effect between chemical and conscious state but a servo-system containing feedback loops both negative and positive.

Religion and Altered States

Mood-altering is very close to the metanoia – change of consciousness – which St Paul defined as the goal of Christianity, but which is, in fact, the broad goal of all religion. It is in the specific goals and methods that religions differ, and where they may be judged for their value. By way of example, where Paul preached that the object of his religion was to "take on the mind that was in Christ"[2], Hinduism preaches it as "Krishna consciousness" and Buddhism as "the Buddha mind." The ways through which different religions seek to change consciousness are diverse, and would suggest the need for a taxonomy of methods, which will not be attempted here, though the following few examples may suffice to make the point initially. Whereas all mainstream Christian churches makes use of hymn-singing, sermons and ecclesiastical art as aids to spiritual experience, so-called "high church" Christianity employs incense, candles and liturgical drama in addition. These are deliberately rejected by Methodism, while Quakers go the extreme, and insist on silence and bare, unadorned meeting houses. Hinduism has its own devices, and the Kama Sutra is unique in attempting to integrate sexual pleasure into religion. Worth particular mention perhaps, is the fact that while stained glass and statuary play a large part in Christianity, Islam rejects pictorial art on principle and relies solely on geometrical designs for religious inspiration. As a fascinating footnote, the great mathematician Hermann Weyl, found examples in Islamic art from centuries ago of all the major symmetries which topologists have only recently discovered through hard logical reasoning.[3] Islamic commentators regard representational art as at best a distraction and at worst a temptation to idolatry, whereas they see the art of geometrical symmetry as an expression of balance, completion and perfection. This raises radical issues in the field of art and spirituality, which can only be noted here.

From the perspective of chemotheology one obvious question is whether psychogenic chemicals produce temporary alterations in consciousness or permanent change in character. There is a wide body of opinion that would argue that taking some substances, especially cannabis and LSD, creates a genuinely spiritual awareness with lasting effects, of which Aldous Huxley's The Doors of Perception is probably the best known. In his words, "To be shown for a few timeless hours the outer and inner world … as apprehended by Mind at Large is an experience of inestimable value to everyone and especially to the intellectual." [4] Although he says that "the man who comes back through the Door in the Wall will … be wiser but less sure, happier but less self-satisfied, humbler in acknowledging his ignorance," there is, in general, little emphasis on the use of drugs to expand ethical awareness. This is a serious lack, for spiritual development must surely be coterminous with growth in moral sensitivity. Huxley's work was pioneering in many ways and would serve as a valuable introduction to chemotheology, but as a record of his own experience in taking mescaline to expand and intensify awareness, it raises as many questions as it answers. While one can easily appreciate the value of experiencing an intense feeling of wonderment at the vividness of colours or patterns in familiar things (such as the folds of his trousers which he cites as an example), the ultimate significance is open to question, not to mention the "bad trips" that are an unavoidable hazard. There is no shortage of data on the effects of psychedelic drugs; rather, the problem may be in organizing it significantly.

The prophylactic use of drugs in the cause of developing spiritual awareness overlaps considerably with their psychogenic use. One could hardly argue, for instance, against taking an aspirin or other analgesic, even opioids, to cure a disabling headache, in order to restore a normally receptive state of consciousness. Here chemotheology treads a fine line, for cannabis has well recognized therapeutic effects in some medical conditions, but rolling a spliff to calm one's nerves does not seem to be much different from enjoying a cigarette or gin and tonic as far as relevance to spirituality is concerned.

Spiritual Highs and Lows

From the perspective of chemotheology, the honest seeker after truth must ask if the search for God – to put it oversimply – is not at base the search for a kind of chemical pleasure, like the jogger's adrenaline high. The case against religion is even more damning if one accepts that the God hypothesis is a fantasy. This is essentially the case argued by Richard Dawkins and other secularists, but must be bypassed here in order to focus on the aspect of chemical pleasure. It should, however, be said that cosmology gives at least as much support to belief in a creation event, as to the hypothesis as "it all just happened." The fact that one gains pleasure from religious activities does not automatically make them self-serving. The principle at issue is far more complex than that, for in general nature organizes things so that we obtain pleasure from doing what is needed for survival of the species and the individual. A nursing mother, for instance, may obtain pleasurable feelings from her body producing the hormone oxytocin, but this does not make breast-feeding her baby a selfish activity in a negative sense. So while it would be true to say that religious practices are designed to produce pleasurable feelings at various levels, from smells to bells, as colloquially expressed, the critical issue is whether the pleasure stops at that level or is in some way a preparation for, and inducement to seek, a higher, more spiritual level of emotional satisfaction.

For the greater part of our history humans have behaved compulsively under the influence of adrenaline, testosterone and oestrogen. These major chemicals have generated the aggressive urges and sexual drives which once helped us to survive but are now at odds with civilization and indeed with survival of the species. We are enslaved to the ancient gods of war and what Arthur Koestler called "the tyranny of the gonads." Tribal aggression is now on a continental scale and runaway population increase is stripping the globe of food and water resources, not to mention others such as timber and metals. What we need now is some way to selectively turn off the lower brain centres, which are the seat of the automatic fight or flight reflex, and the hardly less automatic sexual and maternal drives, and turn on the higher brain centres. The higher brain refers particularly to the prefrontal cortex, which is not only the source of ethical feelings but the control centre for the whole brain.[5] We must now learn how to use this master lobe of the brain to control the production and flow of neurochemicals in the cause of evolution and individual fulfilment.

Chemotheology is a whole new continent to be explored in pursuit of this goal. At present we do not know what value it will have for either science or religion, nor do we have reliable maps. There are several possible beachheads on which to make a landing, one of the most promising being to extend the concept of homeostasis from the body's physical system to consciousness.

Finding the Balance

Homeostasis is a significant concept because it indicates dynamic balance, continually shifting, and in this respect differs from the balance of stasis. A wooden cube sitting on a table has the perfect balance of stasis, as against a tightrope walker, who maintains balance by many bodily adjustments, some deliberate but most unconscious. Individual growth and human evolution depend on homeostasis at several levels. From a neurochemical point of view, habitual consciousness is kept in balance by maintaining an optimum level of serotonin in the brain. Serotonin sometimes called "the happiness molecule", is a key neurotransmitter, enabling electrical currents to bridge the synaptic gaps, and thus maintain an optimum flow of the neural energy that generates consciousness. As an agent of transmission, keeping the neural currents flowing, it might be compared roughly to the oil without which a mechanical transmission will not function. Too low a level of serotonin leaves us in varying degrees feeling depressed, deprived in a undefinable way, listless, fearful and ill at ease with our self and with the world in general.

Sometimes the deprivation may have an obvious cause, such as lack of love or of food, but there are less obvious deprivations which arise from the very nature of being human. Leaving aside spiritual needs, which have been called "the divine discontent," we exist as members of a community, from which we take our identity and our sense of the purpose of life, and as community breaks down, both these factors become problematical. We exist not as pebbles on a beach but as cells in a body, and serotonin balance depends on relationships, from individual to global. We are organic parts of greater wholes, from the family, through the nation, to the human species. Their welfare is our welfare. To the extent that we are empathic, we suffer as they suffer and rejoice as they rejoice. Not all feel this way, by any means, but it is surely a mark of the fully human person. The extreme individualism of Western culture in our time has brought with it a dilemma in which the need for individual freedom is at odds with the need to be part of a community. To the extent that one experiences these needs, serotonin levels will be less than optimal, and we feel not fully alive.

Physicians and psychiatrists alleviate short term lack of serotonin with Prozac and Valium, but because the serotonin level is related to blood sugar level, the individual will often seek a quick fix by taking sugar. Chocolate is the great comforter, and in the context of spiritual needs, it is instructive that John's Gospel refers continually to the Holy Spirit as the comforter, for belief in what has been called "invisible means of support" would seem to fall in the category of self-generated serotonin production. The action of chocolate in raising serotonin levels comes not primarily from sugar but from the fact that it contains several chemicals which generate subtle alterations in mood. Indeed, the range of these mood-altering substances and the complexity of their effects has given rise to what is sometimes called "the science of chocolate." The two best known of them are probably tryptophan and phenylethylamine, which, in stimulating the production of serotonin, appear to mimic the effects of human love. In this connection, a friend once described to me the effect of a successful group meditation, which she said was like having warm chocolate poured over her. This startling image highlights the question raised earlier about the goal of religious practice: in a nutshell, does meditation – solitary or in a group – risk becoming a search for selfish pleasure, albeit of a non-material kind? The very real possibility of de-spiritualizing religion by stopping at the level of the sensory is well exemplified in the Russian Orthodox liturgy, where clouds of incense, candlelight, icons replete with gold leaf, rich vestments, and powerful choirs can provide quite overwhelming pleasure, even to atheists.

Serotonin also plays an intriguing role in bridging mind and matter, insofar as it is produced not only by direct chemical action but by thought. We can overcome mild depression by taking thought (e.g., imagining an impending happy event), and medical science is starting to take seriously the wider therapeutic implications of this phenomenon.[6] Understandably, allopathic medicine is strongly opposed to programmes in which "positive thinking" is prescribed as a therapy, and the experimental data that exists is ambiguous enough to suggest that the facts are largely determined by what one wants to believe. There is, however, no doubt that serotonin destroys cancer cells in vitro,[7] which suggests that there is some correlation between serotonin levels and cancer, which raises all manner of interesting questions as to what makes serotonin toxic in this situation, and how the knowledge can be applied clinically.

In the broad view, serotonin is produced

- *as a physical response when hunger and sexual needs are satisfied,*
- *as an emotional response when there is love,*
- *as an intellectual response when curiosity is resolved, and*
- *as a spiritual response when one's need for experience of the "divine other" is satisfied.*

Clearly, there is a massive agenda here for analysis of all the factors which come together to create the fully satisfied individual, but the significance of homeostasis in mental and physical wellbeing is, paradoxically, that the fully human person is never completely satisfied. He or she must always be in a state of challenge, and when no natural challenge is there, we have a need to create one. To this end we invent sports and games of all kinds. A jigsaw puzzle is a perfect example of the paradox of this aspect of homeostasis, seemingly without purpose, but enjoyable simply for the sake of experiencing the challenge. This line of approach to homeostasis leads us to ask what constitutes a spiritual challenge, such that we have a meaningful goal in view and habitual motive to pursue it.

Eustress, Distress and Practical Chemotheology

Walter Cannon's trail-blazing work *The Wisdom of the Body*[8] not only introduced the term and concept of homeostasis but opened up new medical vistas by showing the physical and mental effects of extreme or prolonged stress, and in particular the devastating effect on both mind and body when the fight or flight reflex is blocked. Twenty five years later Hans Selye's *The Stress of Life* [9] took our understanding to a new level by pursuing the logic of homeostasis to what now seems in retrospect an obvious conclusion, namely that if the healthy body is to avoid stasis – for stasis is vegetation and total stasis is death – some degree of stress is not only healthy but essential. It is therefore vital to distinguish between constructive stress, which generates serotonin, and destructive stress which depletes it.

Selye contrasted them by inventing the term "eustress", which is beneficial, and not to be confused with distress. The two extremes can be found in religion, as in many other aspects of life. Eustress in religion is a field almost totally unexplored, yet for lack of understanding the principle, religious experience can be debilitating rather than vitalizing. Most obviously, in the field of ethics, a sense of right and wrong, which is vital in personal development and human evolution, can easily deform into feelings of guilt and sinfulness, and this has become a bane in Christianity, even more perhaps in Judaism, which has been described as "systematized angst." Spiritual distress is routinely and mistakenly elevated over eustress. One instance which is worth particular note is that in Christianity, and rather differently in Islam, the eustress of spiritual challenge has been expressed very often in images of warfare, and the literature is replete with phrases that echo it – Onward, Christian soldiers, The sword of the spirit, Fight the Good Fight, etc., not to mention the concepts of crusade and jihad. Scupoli's *Spiritual Combat*, written in the sixteenth century, is still in print. Without being too critical of an earlier age when more robust, even warlike, metaphors were called for, it can at least be asked whether they have outlived their value and contribute to religious aggression more than they do to spiritual growth.

The need to keep dynamic balance in habitual consciousness, which goes along with neurochemical balance, suggests that the spiritual challenge needs a better metaphor than constant warfare. Knowing that spiritual capacity should not be overstrained at any stage of development puts one in mind of ship being drawn by a tug, which seeks optimum tension in the tow-rope. Too little and there is drift, too much and the rope breaks. By analogy, too challenging a spiritual discipline and the vital tension snaps, motivation disappears in failure and the balance between incentive and capability is destroyed. If chemotheology can play even a small part in keeping that vital hawser of the spiritual challenge intact, its value will be beyond question.

First Conclusions

The first draft of this paper was embarked upon very speculatively, but comments and questions from a few friends made clear that serious issues about morality, spirituality, religious practice and the human sciences lay just beneath the surface of the theme, too many, in fact, to be properly addressed in a short paper.

The overarching question was whether or not something of real theological and spiritual value could be obtained by showing how spiritual consciousness is linked at a physiological level with chemicals. The linkage is complex, and has necessarily been over-simplified here; yet I hope the fact that it has been shown to exist adds a new dimension to a scientific theology and, particularly, to understanding the spiritual challenge. A knowledge of mood-altering chemicals will not make us more spiritual, but it can make us reflect on the meaning of the word "spirituality," which seems to be taken in general as an all-purpose good, vaguely opposed to materialism, but able to coexist quite comfortably with selfishness. It can also help turn our minds towards an almost forgotten question – what is the point of religion? What use is it if it does not enable the individual and the species to unlock and develop their latent potential to become more human?

If it be assumed that the human species will continue to evolve, then its evolutionary potential must include the capacity for future development of spiritual awareness. On this assumption, chemotheology can be seen to throw new light on fundamental questions that will give us better understanding of where we ought to go, how to get there and what is possible. It has something of importance to say about the age-old problem of freewill, in that knowing how our states of mind and behaviour are governed by neurochemicals will help the spiritual seeker to avoid guilt or depression when he or she falls short of the ideal. It will help too in distinguishing between self-centred spirituality, which is no spirituality at all, and authentic spirituality where a decentring of self – call it love – is slowly seen to be the purpose of life. These surely are benefits, worth having.

References

1. Patricia Churchland, as reported by her husband Paul, and fellow psychoscientist, from an interview with both in *The New Yorker*, Feb. 12, 2007. p. 69.

2. Phillippians 2:5, and elsewhere.

3. Hermann Weyl, *Symmetry*. Princeton UP, 1983.

4. Aldous Huxley, *The Doors of Perception*. NY: Harper Collins, 2004 [1932]. p. 28.

5. cf. Oliver Sacks and Elkhonon Goldberg, *The Executive Brain: Frontal Lobes and the Civilized Mind*. NY: OUP, 2004.

6. cf. John Illman and Rita Carter, *Use Your Brain to Beat Depression*. London: Cassell, 2004.

7. J. Stephenson, "Burkitt's Lymphoma Suicide Can Be Driven by Serotonin," *Lancet Oncology*. vol 3, no. 5, 1 May 2003. p. 265.

8. Walter Cannon, *The Wisdom of the Body*. NY: Norton, 1932.

9. Hans Selye, *The Stress of Life*. NY: McGraw-Hill, 1956.

Part 4:

STRIKING OUT

It should be self-evident that since there is a single creating power, the future towards which religion should strive must be based on a unified view of this power. In practice, however, the ideal is abandoned because the great faith groups are not seriously concerned with a world suffering spiritual hunger but with protecting the theologies that they have inherited from the past. Ecumenism is the thinnest of veneers on religious turf wars.

The first of the two essays in this part takes the term *entheism* as an indicator of the kind of unified theology that the worlds of science and religion now need, and gives reasons in justification. In an incomplete form entheism has been taught by isolated individuals in many religious traditions. The argument here is that by setting it within the new world view of science, and taking it from the margin to the centre of religion, a major step in human evolution is made possible.

The second piece is a plea to raise religious sights above past tribalisms, however noble, and set them on the needs of the global family. The aim of the paper can be expressed as a question: what sort of religion is needed to create the kind of unity that the term "global family" implies?

FROM PANTHEISM TO ENTHEISM

What guides the evolution of an organism, or species of organism, for whom physical survival is no longer a practical issue? What is to drive our future evolution? For thousands of years sages of the East have spoken of "Evolution of the spirit." It is a course remarkably different from that identified by Darwinian thought. They called it "annihilation of self." [1]

The Evolutionary Spiral

The religion of society around us is the matrix within which personal spirituality develops, and thus when an individual feels called to go beyond what might be called the religious norm, tension between religion and spirituality is inevitable. From this perspective, spirituality may be considered the primary element, and defining it becomes a first challenge. What actually is a spiritual person? How is one recognized? Is spirituality a universal, a cultural or even a genetic thing? Is it related to intelligence? What are its benefits? Does it have a downside? Such questions multiply, and there is serious work ahead to answer them if human evolution is assumed to have a spiritual vector. There will, of course, be those who would not accept this assumption at all, and would prefer to replace "spiritual" with "ethical" or "aesthetic" or some more religiously neutral criterion, but I am assuming here that all spirituality contains a "god-component" of some kind. It is this which makes it different from love of nature and the appreciation of art, music or poetry.

Religious evolution rarely happens in a linear fashion, for a newly discovered spiritual truth, which will later become the seed of religious revolution, can only be brought into clear focus if an old truth is put into the background and thus its significance minimized or even denied. Something of the old must die if the new is to be born, but what history shows very often is that an old, discarded principle can later be re-accepted into the system with heightened awareness of its importance. Discovery made at a higher level of understanding is rediscovery, and a new source of both awe and humility.

This pattern of progress can be observed in many aspects of social change, but nowhere so clearly as in the evolution of religion. It may appear superficially to be a restatement of the Hegelian dialectic (thesis > antithesis > synthesis) but the evolutionary impetus lends itself to modelling naturally as a spiral of progress, turning upward, so that in time truths that once were left behind can be seen, as with an eagle's eye view, more sharply and in relation to other truths. As against the almost geometrical principle of the Hegelian dialectic, the evolutionary spiral gives a dynamic awareness, preparing those who understand it to be drawn into the evolutionary process, to know themselves as part of it and feel the imperative to take it forward.

From this perspective what I have called a crossroads in the title of the book can be seen as a place where one may expect old truths to be rediscovered with new significance. The next turn in the spiral, I am proposing, which is already happening in an uncoordinated and fumbling way, will take us to entheism. The word is not in the dictionary, although its root meaning is evident in the *em* of empathy and the *theos* of theology, and the rest of this paper will be devoted to showing why the new word is needed to denote new awareness of an old spiritual insight and to indicate that it will be at once an intellectual and spiritual awareness, and in both cases more demanding and fulfilling than conventional ideas of religion. To the extent that *entheism* labels something genuinely new, understanding its meaning and feeling its significance will not come in a few paragraphs, and this is just a first attempt. Its link to our human past can be appreciated by going back to the very origin of spiritual consciousness.

When all the World was One

There was a time in our history when religious division did not exist, and all humans had the same type of spiritual consciousness, and felt no compulsion to go to war to defend tribal orthodoxies. This happy state existed for 99% of humankind's existence, if we date the emergence of *Homo sapiens* to the invention of fire, about 1.5 million years ago, the best current estimate. From then until three or four thousand years ago most of our forebears led a hunting existence, and we can say with reasonable confidence that they had the kind of spiritual awareness which comparative theology calls primal religion or animism, and which exists still today in primitive hunting communities. Insofar as an archaic type of spiritual awareness can be reconstructed, it seems to have been a sense of oneness with nature and of awe in the face of the forces of nature. This habitual state of consciousness was called *participation mystique* by the ethnologist Lucien Lévy-Bruhl, thus drawing attention to a felt oneness with a creating and life-giving power, which went by different names, such as "Manitou", "mana" and "The Great Spirit," and within which one lived, as if immersed.

It was not a divine power as understood today, however, since it was not thought of as external to the world or personified. What we think of as "God" today is quite different from the Great Spirit of primal religion, which was a force within nature and, for that reason, could be called a natural force. It was, at the same time, however, a super-natural force insofar as it not only made the plants to grow and rivers to run but caused lightning and thunder above the earthly realm. This sense of a life-giving and life-sustaining reality did not carry any ethical implications, other than the imperative to care for and reverence the earth, as is often noted by anthropologists. It is perhaps not too fanciful to think of our preliterate hunting ancestors as Franciscan in spirit, feeling kinship with animals and trees and with "brother sun and sister moon."

By contrast, the hypothesized divinity of the Abrahamic religions (Judaism, Christianity and Islam) is a quasi-personal entity whose abode is above the clouds, who created all things out of nothing "by his word" and, as regards man's relationship with nature, gave instructions to "subdue it, and rule over ... every living thing that moves upon the earth" (*Genesis* 1:30). As the new "god" replaced the old, the individual's sense of oneness with the natural world not only diminished, but was tabooed by the priestly caste who had replaced the shamans in the new order of things, for the two religious perceptions - God inside or outside nature – were mutually exclusive. This distant and external Power is essentially the understanding of divinity which is now being rejected in the West, and it is of no small interest that many of those who reject it have adopted a stylized Druidism and Native American religion in their quest for authentic spiritual experience.

The Great Divide

It is tempting to over-romanticize primal religion, ignoring its serious religious deficits. During this long period, our ancestors by and large lacked a clear sense of their distinctiveness as humans, and the ethical imperative was dim and poorly defined. There is evidence from ancient Indian murals, for instance, that sexual intercourse with animals was not regarded as so abnormal as it would be today, and the fact that the Old Testament fulminates against it as "an abomination before the Lord" in *Leviticus* and elsewhere (cf. *Ezekiel* 16:2) would suggest that it was a serious issue in Jewish society for some centuries. The transition from animistic to ethical religion was a long and winding road, and, as the Bible records, there were many backtrackings.

The history of Judaism is a fascinating story, once one goes beyond the childish belief that it came into being when God handed his ten commandments to Moses on top of Mount Sinai. Modern Scholarship has now revealed how Judaism began as a reaction to an Egyptian religion based on half-human, half-animal divinities, a religion obsessed with survival in an afterlife, and possessing nothing that might be called a moral theology. The ethical monotheism of the Jewish religion marked a 180 degree turn in all these respects. It set human and animal clearly apart, forbidding the ingestion of the blood of animals to avoid the risk of partaking of their spirit. This aspect of the "kosher," or purity, principle endures still among Jews, and was later adopted by Moslems in the "halal" method of preparing meat. Against this historical background it can be seen that drinking the symbolic blood of Jesus in the Eucharistic rite of Roman Catholicism expresses the same ancient belief that we become what we eat, but in this case absorbing the spirit of Jesus is, of course, considered to be good – indeed, the be-all and end-all of Christianity. Judaism stood out starkly from every other religion of its era in being so solidly centred on ethical awareness, based on a vision of man as a moral creature and on a God who was real and in some sense "human". For any communication to take place, say between a human and a dog, there must be, as Aquinas put it, a "connaturality," and so too between God and man. Perhaps the greatest divide between science and religion today is belief or otherwise that communication between the human and divine is possible. It is, need one say, a very serious question, but the fact that an answer is not subject to quantification or other scientific controls does not necessarily prove its impossibility.

The Jewish religion was uncompromising in its conviction that real communication with a real divinity was possible: the prophets, a new kind of shaman, were not communicating with nature but walking and talking with God, something which would be unthinkable in myth-based or idol-based religions. A Greek, for instance, could not imagine communing personally with Zeus or Aphrodite, nor a Roman with Jupiter or Mars. At the same time, it must be noted that for the Jews this intercourse was mainly between God and the tribe, not the individual. That the Jewish god was made in man's image is only to be expected, but what is fascinating is that he was made in the image of an idealised human being. Their God was a "God of truth" and a "God of holiness," so that it was quite natural for Jesus to say, "Be perfect, as your father in heaven is perfect."

In fact, the Jews' mental image of God evolved along with the religious sensitivity of the Jews themselves, changing over a period of some 1,300 years from being a rather ruthless and capricious tyrant to a stern judge and then to the loving father that Jesus felt and preached. But with that, Jewish theology ran out of road: the model of a patriarchal, law-enforcing divinity was developable no further. The original ten commandments had expanded to over three hundred officially recognized laws for right living, and the effect of this on the serious truth-seeker can be imagined. The observant Jew was one who kept all these laws, and the model of the ideal human was deformed into a nitpicking, censorious neurotic. The gospels record Jesus making this point by harsh criticism of the Pharisees, but he also said that he was totally committed to a religion based on the concept of divine law and would not, as the King James Bible puts it, change "one jot or tittle" of it. Like so many Christians today, Jesus was clearly torn between the religion he had inherited and a new spiritual perception that struggled to be born, but was unable to escape. When all is said and done, no criticism of ancient Judaism should blind us to its enormous evolutionary significance. Western civilization stands on the shoulders of the Jewish prophets, and humankind owes them a unique debt of gratitude in taking forward the basic conviction of Judaism, that man was an ethical animal. On the very first page of the Old Testament we read that those who know right from wrong will be "as gods." Under the surface of that hyperbole are hidden depths of wisdom.

The Christian Breakaway

The spiral of religious evolution – or, more precisely here, of the Judaic religious phylum - turned again as Christianity emerged. Christianity was still deeply ethical in spirit, but the Law which had been carved on tablets of stone was now internalised and contextualised, "written in the heart", as Jeremiah (31:33) had foreseen and yearned for. As against orthodox Judaism, which did not believe in life after death, Christianity was squarely centred on belief in survival after death, preached it as the reward for righteousness in this life and "proved" its existence through belief that Jesus had risen from the dead and continued to exist in heaven. Religion thus became again "other-worldly". Christianity was also a reversion in having a human sacrifice at its centre, insofar as the death of Jesus was interpreted as a self-oblation to his divine father god to win forgiveness for the sins of humankind. It all fitted neatly into Paul's half-Jewish, half-Hellenistic theology of scapegoats and sacrificial redemption, and had enormous logical appeal in an earlier age, when hardly anyone was even literate, let alone educated. To modern minds it is gruesome and illogical, but is not questioned by the orthodox Christian, for it is a brick that is keyed into a total theological edifice, and to take it out would risk collapsing the whole. A good number of Protestant hymns, which celebrate redemption through the "blood of the lamb" would be drained of sense, and the Mass and Eucharist would lose their meaning if the re-enacted sacrifice and symbolic partaking of the "body, blood, soul and divinity of Christ" were to be abandoned now.

It cannot be too strongly emphasized how resistant any religion is to the most reasonable criticism, for there is always subliminal awareness that to remove or radically change one piece would collapse a system of thought which has become for its members a mode of self-identification. Religionists know who they are and what is the meaning of life through beliefs that were usually wired in when they were very young, during the developmental period that Piaget called the pre-logical phase of learning, and precisely because it is pre-logical, this wiring is almost impossible to reach thereafter through logical argument. It hardly needs to be emphasized that losing one's sense of identity is, quite literally, a kind of death, so it is no wonder that a radically new theological insight will be resisted violently. It is worth noting, in this regard, how the Jews attempted to assassinate Paul for "attacking our people, our Law and our temple" (Acts 21:28), for they saw his gentilized form of what might be called "Jesus-ism" as a threat to their tribal identity. When the time comes for spirituality and religion to make the next evolutionary step, we can be sure that all the Christian churches, despite the differences which keep them apart, will find a passionate solidarity in resisting what is now seeking to be born, for it will seem to all as a mortal threat.

Rediscovering Sacrifice

The role of sacrifice in theistic religions is age old. It springs from a naïve belief that one can propitiate or bribe a creating divinity by destroying on its behalf something that one values – as if my loss must equate with the god's gain. The sacrificial mentality operates with a simple calculus: the more costly the sacrifice, the greater the potential benefit. Within this context of thought, to obtain the most needed gifts from God called for the greatest sacrifice, and what more valuable than one's child. Human sacrifice was used in many cultures, especially in times of exceptional need, such as famine or threat of invasion, but child-sacrifice seems to have been a peculiarly Canaanite thing. At some point, perhaps as late as 400 BC, the Jews made a principled decision to abandon child sacrifice, a momentous event recorded obliquely in the story of Abraham being told by God first to sacrifice his son, and then not to sacrifice him. The Jews were ahead of other religions in this, for human sacrifice was only officially abolished in Rome in 97 AD, and Aztec altars were being drenched daily with human blood fifteen hundred years later when the Spanish conquistadores arrived. The Jews borrowed child sacrifice from their Phoenician neighbours, among whom it seems to have been routine and who took the practice with them wherever they went as traders. At Carthage, their greatest city, archaeologists have discovered the remains of 20,000 children, with every reason to think that they were killed as a religious offering. Many other such graveyards around the Mediterranean have been found, and are called tophets, after the cultic centre and most famous site of child sacrifice. Tophet was originally the name of a place a couple of miles outside the city limits of modern day Jerusalem, just south of the Mount of Zion. It is an intriguing thought that Jerusalem, which had been a hill fort since the Stone Age, and whose strategic value was recognized by a young war lord from the tribe of Judah called David, seems to be some kind of epicentre for both war and religion.

Although physical sacrifice has disappeared from Judaeo-Christianity, the concept of sacrifice runs wide and deep in human psychology, for it goes along with a primitive perception of the creating power, who is felt to be both dangerous and bribe-able. Somehow the loving God of Jesus manages to coexist in Christianity with the ancient, forever demanding God of early Judaism, without the contradiction being noticed. The great act of Roman Catholic liturgy is performed on a stone altar, which is the focal point of every church, and repeated requests to "the God of love" for mercy (*Kyrie Eleison*) mingle with thanks for his accepting the sacrifice of his son to settle the cosmic account of human sinfulness. Protestant Christianity dispensed with the altar, and made the pulpit a new focus, but the value of a sacrificial attitude is still emphasized, sometimes expressed in the epigram," No cross, no crown."

The extraordinary kind of self-sacrifice that Jesus preached and exemplified goes largely unnoticed, partly perhaps because it was such an innovation in its time and partly because it is difficult to understand even today. A note of caution is always required when talking about what Jesus said and did, for, as we now know, so little of the gospels is a literal account of what actually happened, and is often what the gospel writer, or later editors, would have liked him to say, or thought he might have said. This uncertainty is, however, no bad thing, since those sayings which have the "ring of Jesus" are evidence that his message had either been absorbed by his followers or extended, whether or not he had actually uttered the words in question. In any event, the doctrine of Jesus concerns sacrifice of the self, and is encapsulated in his saying, "It is vital to understand that unless the grain of wheat falls into the ground and dies, it bears no fruit .... Whoever loves himself is lost" (John 12:25). This teaching appears in different forms throughout the New Testament, as, for instance, "If a man loses his self for my sake, he will find his true self" (Matt 16:26). The radical significance of this doctrine is rarely appreciated, for it has been worn smooth over the centuries to mean something like, "Don't be selfish." Indeed, if most people were asked what was the great truth taught by Jesus, they would probably reduce it further, to "Do unto others as you would have them do unto you." There is nothing particularly Christian about these moral precepts, or even religious, for that matter. What is particularly, and astonishingly, Christian is the peculiar doctrine of psychological sacrifice which has been pushed to the margin, but which we have good reason to think was central to the message of Jesus.

It is "peculiar" for three reasons, firstly because it is by no means clear what is the "self" that has to die or be lost, and, secondly, it is not immediately obvious why this should be something good. What would be left of me if my self died? The third reason is that losing one's self appears to be a recipe for evolutionary regression. This is immediately apparent when one considers what a struggle humankind has had to reach a level where a robust sense of self – what psychologists call "ego strength" – is the norm. Indeed, if one looks around the globe, one might guess that the great majority of its inhabitants have still not arrived there. This is a wide area for discussion, and to simplify it, I would refer to Julian Jaynes' thesis, already mentioned, that the human being proper only appeared some three thousand years ago with the emergence of a self-awareness previously unknown. Before that time, our ancestors did not feel themselves to be individuals but members of a group, and the thought of an independent self – i.e., with ideas and feelings different from the group - would have been fragile in the extreme, alien and rather scary. Despite the explosion of culture that began in many advanced societies in the late Bronze Age, the individual mind was almost coterminous with the group mind. The way in which self-consciousness, the idea of "MY self," emerged is a fascinating story, not least because in the transition those pioneers who struggled to develop an individual sense of self were, as Jaynes puts it, literally schizophrenic – they lived with two kinds of consciousness and were driven by two wills – and it is logical to expect the pure Christian doctrine of selflessness to induce for a while in its followers a similar split consciousness. The royal road to higher spiritual awareness would seem to lead through thickets of confusion and self-doubt. We in the twenty first century are, however, the beneficiaries of the movement of the Enlightenment in the eighteenth century, which taught ego-strength as a moral principle. Its watchword, *Sapere aude* – dare to know – must be a watchword now for religion, as well as for science. It becomes the springboard for a new advance.

Was Jesus Unique?

Is the spiritual doctrine of self-sacrifice only to be found in the teaching of Jesus? Christians take Jesus to be unique, but is this due simply to lack of knowledge? Can one find self-lessness taught by other teachers and in other religious traditions? The answer to that will prove surprising, and has profound implications for human evolutionary theory. That Jesus stood out as an exceptionally spiritual human being, with great healing powers and radiating a higher type of consciousness, is evident from all the records we have, but what made him so different is a question that has resisted scientific explanation until recently, and a comprehensive analysis awaits some future psycho-theologian. Speculation about the significance of Jesus is evident in the Christian scriptures from the beginning, ranging from the hypothesis that he was a prophet of the rank of Moses and Elijah to the embodiment of the divine Wisdom which had existed from eternity, to the personification of the Logos or word of God. The case was closed at the Council of Nicaea in 325, when the emperor Constantine imposed the opinion of Athanasius on the assembled bishops, and orthodox Christianity is defined today by the limitations of his vision. Jesus is a god come down from heaven, born of a virgin, his body resurrected after death (as befits an eternal god) and he is now back in heaven with his Father. This imposed solution gained peace and unity within the Christian church after half a century of Arian wars (the term is hardly too strong, for many were killed) and provided a robust theology that answered to the needs of a naïve and largely illiterate religious community. The Athanasian theory of Jesus has stood the test of time, but now science and universal education have weakened its structure in every joint.

Among the things that were lost was a critical weakening of the doctrine of self-sacrifice, just noted, on which Jesus placed so much importance, and which is central in the concept of entheism. This doctrine arises from a rare type of consciousness, an intense awareness of the reality of a higher power, and from a decentring of self and change in self-identity that followed from it. How do such rare individuals see themselves and how do they feel? Jesus may be said to have answered these questions in declaring, "To do the will of my father in heaven is my meat and drink" (John 4:34, etc.). It is at the same time a statement of subordination and of love, such as can be found in thousands of popular love songs. Cole Porter put it in alimentary terms too, when he wrote, "You're the cream in my coffee, you're the salt in my soup … I'd be lost without you." The average person's attitude is, by contrast, summed up in the story of the religious lesson in which the teacher asked a bored teenager if she loved God, and received the answer, "Sure, I love God, but I'm not crazy about him." The underlying point is that in a situation of love, there is a shift in self-perception, so that the other, and his or her wishes, becomes more important than my own, and this is a sort of craziness, certainly not normal. One of the most significant episodes in the gospel, and one never preached about, is when the family of Jesus thought he was crazy and tried to put him under restraint (Mark 3:20). This would make complete sense if he was embarrassing the family by teaching a cockeyed doctrine about the death of the self. We do not know, of course, what he was preaching on this occasion, but unselfishness can hardly have been a controversial theme. His doctrine of selflessness is, however, critically different, for we can become very unselfish without attempting to get rid of the self altogether. The term "traumatic" means life-changing, and when Jesus talks of the death of self, it seems clear that he is urging on his listeners not just an intellectual position or acceptance of a new set of rules, but something traumatic in the extreme. Unfortunately, he did not say much about the logistics of self-sacrifice, or at least the gospels do not record it, and this is why Jewish commentators invariably, and sincerely, ask how is the teaching of Jesus different from Judaism.

Everything that Jesus said in the Sermon on the Mount can be found somewhere, and often repeatedly, in the Old Testament. The difficulty in identifying what was new arises from the fact that a religion dedicated to the pursuit of selflessness conflicts with a religion dedicated to keeping the Law. So Jesus, as a pious Jew, was trying to go in two directions at the same time. His deepest spiritual intuition was at odds with his native religion, from which there was no escape, at least until Paul, the Graeco-Roman Jew came on the scene. He did not so much find the key as smash the lock. Jesus would have been utterly horrified to have been told that "those who rely on obedience to the Law are under a curse" (*Galatians* 3:10).

The Non-Uniqueness of Jesus

Once one sees Jesus not as a one-off but as an evolutionary fore-runner, a biological holotype, it is not so startling to discover many other individuals who shared with him the same kind dual awareness of self. Indeed, the most ancient spiritual teaching of Hinduism, predating Jesus by a thousand years, is based on the principle of Advaita, or "not-twoness," and is orthodox teaching today, but has on the whole become swamped with a popular polytheism. From this historical perspective, in preaching the vital importance of self-sacrifice Jesus was reinventing the wheel, and looking further, one can see that this particular wheel has been reinvented many times in many ages and in many societies. It is, in fact, so universal in religious culture that it is often referred to as the perennial philosophy, but the term is risky, since it implies a purely rational understanding, whereas self-sacrifice – when the stress is put on "sacrifice" – is much more than a philosophical position.

It is clear from the quotations below that the authors are talking of something deeply emotional, but something disturbing and challenging as well as blissful. What is deeply significant is that, if one removes the cultural context (such as the Christian "Father" and the Moslem "Allah") the thoughts expressed could have come from within any theistic tradition.

> The Father and I are one. Who sees me sees the Father. (Jesus, a Jew)

> I am He whom I love, and He whom I love is I .... If thou seest me, thou seest him. (Al Hallaj, Moslem)

> This is your real Self, the Supreme Being .... Who does not look for liberation in the Divine Self is deluded and grasps at the unreal. Knowing reality is awakening to the unity of the Divine Self. (Shankara, Hindu)

> Where I am, there is God. (Meister Eckhart, Christian)

> Between Thou and me there stands an "I". O Allah, of Thy mercy take away this "I". (Abu Said, Moslem)

> The world teems with idols for us to break, but as long
> as you exist as a self, there is one more idol left to break.
> (Iqbal, Moslem)

> The true nature of all self-denial is to break down that
> which stands between God and us. (William Law, Chris-
> tian)

Such expressions can be found in thousands, if one cares to seek, but
all are classified and routinely dismissed as "mysticism" and thus not
of central importance in religion, and again I return to the insistence
of Jesus that in his perception of religion, this self-transformation is
vitally important, for this is a statement of the crossroads at which
religion in general now finds itself.

One must decide whether the type of self-consciousness illustrated
above is anomalous, an evolutionary aberration, a mysterious seventh
sense (rather like synaesthesia), which will always be for the few or,
on the other hand, an evolutionary challenge which until now humankind has not been able to meet. I would argue that selflessness,
in the extreme form preached by Jesus and other, as just quoted, is
a higher form of consciousness towards which human evolution has
been groping almost blindly, but which now must be sought with
eyes wide open. If this book has one thing to say, it is that science is
now opening our eyes to the possibility of the abnormal becoming
normal. Once it is seen as a possibility, it becomes an imperative. To
take the phrase of the religious philosopher Ernst Troeltsch, which
he used in regard to historical theology, give it your finger and it will
take your hand.

The Turn of Entheism

I will propose that the next turn of the spiral of religious evolution will
take us to a clearer understanding of Jesus's death-of-self doctrine by
returning us at a higher level to the self-less-ness of primal religion,
that is, to an habitual sense of *participation*. There will however be
critical differences between entheism, as here outlined, and what
Jesus and others have taught. It will be clear from the brief words
above that the next turn of the spiral will take us to a place that is,
in one very important sense, post-Christian, but it will equally be
post-Jewish, post-Moslem and post-Hindu. The evolutionary spiral
is a very grand narrative, and will probably be confusing to anyone
who is not able to stand back a long way and look at religion on a

global and very long historical scale. The critical differences between entheism and what could easily be dismissed as mysticism are essentially three. Entheism will

- be inseparable from the creation story that science is now revealing

- entail both the expansion and intensification of normal human awareness

- have a logistical, rather than logical, foundation.

As regards the new creation story, enough has been said already to indicate that a cosmogony which reaches the conclusion that our universe began as a point of energy in hyperspace cannot avoid the logical corollary that all that now exists was once "within" that point. The scientific and theological consequences of that postulate will need a long time to tease out but once accepted – for scientific reasons – it follows that our universe is not a closed energetic system. From a theological perspective, it follows that all that exists is within "God" and "God" is within everything. It will be clear why the quotation marks are required, for this is far from the Abrahamic religions' understanding of the Creating Power (Hinduism is a different and more complex case.) The end of this reasoning may be stated, oversimply, as the normalisation of mystical awareness in religion. This point has been made by Karl Rahner and others.

As regards the expansion and extension of consciousness which is the main aim of entheism, and its *sine qua non*, the intellectual and emotional aspects will be inseparable in several respects. Understanding of entheism can be pursued through various forms of study, but these will be only a preliminary, like the first stage of a rocket which must be discarded when it has served its usefulness. The main objective of entheism, and its *raison d'être*, is the expansion of empathic awareness, in three dimensions:

i. an empathy with our fellow humans, a sharing of their consciousness, so that our different selves move closer together, towards a kind of shared self. This is the same as, but more than, "love thy neighbour." It means something like "get inside his head, share his feelings, double his joy, halve his sorrow." It calls for work, loving sometimes through gritted teeth.

   ii.   an empathy with what might be called "God in nature," for in feeling our oneness with the natural world, we are united with the same spirit by which it lives. As Thomas Traherne wrote three centuries ago, "You never enjoy the world aright, till the sea itself floweth in your veins ... and you perceive yourself to be the sole heir of the whole world." Reaching this state will call for new (and old) ways of learning to see and feel beauty in nature, but it is far more than aesthetics, for the world is full of ugliness and evil as well as life and beauty.

   iii. an empathy with humanly created beauty – music, art and poetry, most obviously. It is surely the most scandalous failure of education in general that most individuals probably leave school with no more power to absorb and resonate with the beauty of the world than when they entered. What kind of world could we create if everyone knew and loved the same great musical pieces, and works of art and literature. That would surely be a giant step towards realising a global family.

Within an entheistic understanding, all this is but "prologue to a swelling act," which might be called empathy with the divine, the direct and naked sense of presence, which may be approached but is ultimately given, and can only be waited for. This is more than pantheism, or even Karl Krause's panentheism, the essence of which is expressed in the Hindu saying *Tat tuam asi* – Thou art that. Entheism, as simple awareness of the Ultimate Existent, is in a strange way almost the opposite, an awareness expressible in the phrase "That Thou art," which is about as close as one can get to wordlessness.

How Important a Crossroads?

Animism today is for those who wish to feel but not to think. For anyone who is concerned with the big questions of life – who were are, where we came from, where we are going to – there are four choices. Atheism, illogical as it may be, is promoted with some passion by individuals such as Richard Dawkins and Christopher Hitchens, but mostly as an antidote to the failures of theism. Agnosticism is adequately catered for by Buddhism, or at least by the Buddhist attitude. Theism is sufficient for those who are satisfied with the concept of a patriarchal divinity and all the doctrines and practices that follow from it. Entheism is for those who are not satisfied, and who accept that a relationship with "God" will ultimately entail a change of identity. Teilhard de Chardin looked forward to a future when humankind has crossed this threshold, when, "for the second time in the history of the world man shall have invented fire." However, just as Jesus was locked into his native Judaism, Teilhard could not escape the intellectual framework of his native Christianity, and just as Judaism, trapped in a religion based on Law, developed by expanding the original principle of ten commandments into three hundred laws, Teilhard's thought developed by expanding belief in the unique divinity of Jesus into an anticipated "emergence of the Cosmic Christ." (One may be grateful that there are no competing cosmic Mohameds or Buddhas.) While I would by no means reject his striking metaphor of reinventing fire, the critical step higher towards which our species is now moving seems to me more comparable in its evolutionary importance to its earliest beginning, when we began to walk on two legs.

We can only speculate on how our distant ancestors first started to branch off from the hominid tree, but certainly we could not have become a tool-using animal without freeing up our front paws to be used as hands. As can be observed by watching apes stand upright for a short time, bipedalism is an unstable, awkward and unnatural state, but something kept our forebears attempting this for a very long period in the past, and during that time losing the skills that had enabled them to live comfortably in the trees. If, in a thought experiment, we can imagine them being shown a film of Jesse Owens or Fred Astaire and Ginger Rogers, they would have found such speed and grace of movement incredible and impossible. In a similar way, individuals in the early 21st century striving towards spiritual fulfilment will find it hard to imagine where a species in pursuit of selflessness will end up. Like our distant ancestors, all we can do is keep on with our spiritual stumbling about.

Somewhere down the road, assuming that our species does not destroy itself and the planet along the way, there will come a general awakening to the fact, emphasized throughout this book, that we are the only species which can decide what it wants to be and, furthermore, that this decision can no longer be avoided. It is a question of an old identity now breaking up and dysfunctional. Jesus and the writers quoted knew intuitively that progress into full humanity involved the emergence of a new kind of self and, necessarily, the death of the old. We may choose at this point to find out more, or we may leave it for future generations to find out and act accordingly. That is the first decision, and the great majority will, without doubt, neither see nor feel any need for it. For those who feel a need for change there will be far more pressure to stay with the familiar and the socially authorized than to start on an unfamiliar and very demanding path. In this situation, the best and most practical advice is to live with the old, comfortable identity as long as one can. The need to make a decision will arise in its own time. Every decision must be personal – there can be nothing comparable to mass baptisms – and different in the detail. The "dying to self" and "losing of self" which Jesus and other visionaries taught will probably be for most a slow and uncertain process culminating in a life-altering decision. For some it will be an enormous psychological wrench, but for others more a letting go, even a relief, like taking off an ill-fitting, grubby and restrictive garment, and finding a new freedom.

Whichever way it happens, the end result must be the recentring of a personal universe, directly comparable to the recentring of the physical universe initiated by Copernican theory. This also began as a personal vision and was at first considered wildly eccentric, wrong-headed and contrary to common observation that the sun went round the earth every day. It was initially rejected by most astronomers and virtually all ordinary people, but once fine-tuned and accepted, it laid the foundation for modern science. As well as being a sacrifice of self and a recentring, radical self-transformation will have physiological consequences, for it will both depend upon and bring about "a dramatic rewiring of neural connections [with] certain precise chemical reactions in specific synaptic clefts .... a re-synapsing of crucial neural connections." The quotation, and the one at the head of this essay, are from Ali Ansari, quoted earlier in the piece "Neurotheology and Freewill." He is a Moslem, a professor of engineering, an ordinary person made extraordinary by his knowledge of Sufism and science and his sense of being part of the great evolutionary stream. The fact that his prophetic words come from another tradition, usually assumed to be antagonistic to Christianity, offers great hope that a new theology is coming to birth which will transcend all religious divisions and in the very long term do away with them. Then the ideal of a global family will become real and attainable.

References

1. Ali Ansari, *Sufism and Beyond: Sufi Thought in the Light of Late 20th Century Science.* Ahmedabad: Mapin Publishing. 2000 pp. 16 & 20-21, slightly adapted.

TOWARDS A UNIFIED AND UNIFYING UNDERSTANDING

I suddenly realized it's all one, that this magnificent universe is a harmonious, directed, purposeful whole, that we humans, both as individuals and as a species, are an integral part of the ongoing process of creation.

Edgar Mitchell, Apollo Astronaut

Truth Mythological and Scientific

As the old religions lose their power to inspire, and thus to take humanity onward and upward, the new creation story now being told by science is illuminating the ancient awareness of God-in-man and opening up a new revelation. The new awareness has the power to unify the fractured human family by transcending all the old myths and bringing everyone together in a common understanding. This new mode of consciousness will have a doubly unifying effect: it will bring together head and heart in the individual and bring people of different cultures together. It will thus release the individual and society from the cognitive dissonance that comes when the eye of ordinary logic and the eye of spiritual intuition look out, so to speak, at two different worlds. Cognitive dissonance numbs thought and feeling, paralyzes action and prevents growth, and something similar happens with whole societies when scientific and prescientific cultures strive to co-exist. Since we cannot find harmony by going back to the past - although fundamentalists in both religion and science attempt to do so - we must press on into the future.

The problem we face today as seekers of truth is that the emerging new vision of science is as yet barely seen and carries no obvious authority, while the great religious myths of the past have historical authority and what one might call tribal validation. Faith communities are, in effect, tribes which take their identity from belief in a particular myth. The great religious and political myths have the psychological power that comes from the felt truth that lies beneath the stories they tell, for no great myth tells a trivial story, and this is at the heart of the world's religious problems. Take, for example, Christianity. The historical truth is that Jesus was executed by the Romans as a political dissident and as a genuine threat to the peace of the region, but the image of a man of suffering and the message of a love that does not count the cost goes deeper into our psyche than any historical fact. The advancement of humanity, therefore, seems to be held back by the almost hypnotic hold which ancient religious and political myths exercise on our creative imagination.

Whether or not we aspire to the scientific attitude, it is now a part of western culture, and therefore those who adhere to religions which require belief in an unhistorical fiction must necessarily run their life by two standards of truth, keeping them in separate compartments of their mind and relying on the fig leaf of a double truth principle to cover the moral issue involved. Once it has been decided that legend and fable are the appropriate and essential forms of truth for religion, there is no limit to the myths that can be created in the name of religious truth. History can be invented with the same ease, and often for much the same reasons of corporate control, as it was reinvented in Soviet Communist school texts. A quite recent example of mythmaking in the cause of religion is the announcement in 1950 by Pope Pius XII of the relocation of the revivified body of the mother of Jesus from earth to "heaven," to be with her son and take her rightful place as the Mother of God. This is now part of the mythology which Roman Catholics must believe, since it was uttered infallibly by the pope, papal infallibility being itself a late-invented myth. Protestant Christians should hesitate before laughing at all this, for their own biblical mythology is hardly less credible in a scientific age. Some thirty million fundamentalists in America believe they will be swept up to heaven with Jesus in "the Rapture" and several polls have revealed that over forty per cent of Americans believe that the world was created in seven days, as the Bible tells. There is no point in multiplying such instances, for the point at issue is whether or not one can realise one's full human potential while trying to maintain a double standard of truth, one of which calls for flat denial of common logic and evidential fact.

A Hub and Spoke Strategy

It is not surprising that many who seek spiritual fulfilment today – not knowing quite what the term means – are held back by their intellectual integrity from joining any established faith. To fulfil their hopes and aspirations a community of individuals is needed, bound together by desire to find a common, convincing and life-transforming truth. A common world view is now needed to replace the conflicting world views of the great religions, for the very latest of them arose when mankind believed that the sun went round the earth. A new world view will be the necessary framework within which a new kind of religious sensitivity can develop, and that world view must be evolutionary.

When it comes to creating a post-Christian, post-Islamic, post-Hindu, post-everything spiritual community the image of a wheel will be helpful. If the hub represents the unity of truth and the spokes our individual journeys, it can easily be appreciated that although spiritual seekers start from different points, and have different temperaments and life experience, if they are genuine truth seekers, all are on converging paths. Most people under the age of forty in the West will have been influenced far more by television programmes than by religious teaching of any kind, and are thus coming from different places. They may have started in one of the ancient religions or from nowhere in particular, but the further that we all travel down our personal "spoke" in our own way and at our own speed, the closer we come to experiencing the common truth and to loving each other, and the greater we feel the convergent pull of genuine community.

Unity in Diversity

We can be sure that if the answer to society's spiritual needs were simple, the religions which now exist, and which have the full weight of authority that comes from long tradition, would have found it already. What we need and what existing religions do not provide are three things which in combination amount to something radically new.

Firstly, we need to develop not only toleration of individual differences but keen awareness that we need them to enable our personal potential to be realised. A herd or flock is defined by uniformity but a true human community today must be created from the consciousnesses of many individuals in dynamic balance, with active acceptance of each member's uniqueness and their need for understanding and support. What is here called "dynamic balance" is in practice essentially old-fashioned love, except that in the modern age we all need physical and psychological space as well as fellowship, and this is something quite new in the history of the social group. In the past, religious communities were defined by a closeness and conformity that is not appropriate today. In an emergent community there will be a need for some time to know where each is "coming from", for we can no longer take for granted that there is a shared cultural background. This is the rationale behind the "hub and spoke" model of a community where unity and uniformity, similarity and difference vitalize instead of deadening the spirit or creating anarchy. It represents no small challenge.

Secondly, we need a rational basis for a contemporary and universal theology, an adult understanding of the creating power to underpin the faith element of religion. At the same time, since most of the world's population still thinks unscientifically, and probably over half are functionally illiterate, there remains still a great need for myth in the form of a simple narrative theology. While the evolutionary story, both cosmic and biological, can be presented in a perfectly simple form, it will need to coexist for a long time with prescientific myth. We are talking here of the grand narratives, for fables of all kinds and on all scales have a permanent role in communicating wisdom, and so long as we are clearly aware that they are fictional and educational, they have an invaluable role to play in human development. If the concept of myth and symbol is extended and, so to speak, dynamized, to include music, drama, art, dance and poetry, it can be argued that new art forms of many kinds are now required to fulfil the essential role that myth plays in creating culture and identity. We must neither underestimate the power of symbol and myth to effect us at a subconscious level nor overlook the fact that the story told by science is itself a kind of mythology, based on certain acts of faith about reality. These are, however, rational and testable acts of faith, and therein lies their religious significance.

Thirdly, a unified theology, however it is to be defined, must be developmental in spirit and form. It cannot be just an intellectual system, but must incorporate motivational elements that will bring about self-transformation as the system is learned and internalized, in effect, wired into our consciousness. The truth of any religion must be clearly seen to lie in its ability to change us, give us a new kind of happiness and ultimately to carry society to a higher evolutionary level.

A Sense of Presence

Since a unified theology takes as its goal the experience of God, it may be considered, by comparison with the norm, as mystical. However, although it would be accurate to say that it seeks mystical experience as a higher kind of religious norm, this is essentially an habitual, if intermittent, sense of presence, which might be compared with the awareness that a mother has of her child, whether or not it be physically present. Although never referred to as such, maternal awareness really is an altered state in comparison with what might be considered the norm. For the first time mother, of course, it is a new norm. It is vital not to confuse spirituality as an habitual altered state with the ecstasies, bliss and rapture that many regard as evidence of higher states of consciousness. Bernini's famous statue of Saint Teresa of Avila in a state of almost orgasmic swoon has done true religion no service at all in making the experience of God seem to be so exotic and exaggerated. We may get a better idea of what we should be aiming towards by reading the poets - Wordsworth, Hopkins, Eliot, Rilke, Herbert, Keats Blake and others too many to mention. Their gift lies in finding the telling image where reflection and emotion fuse. They help us to go beyond all religious dogma and to see "infinity in a grain of sand" and an "earth crammed with heaven and every common bush afire with God."

At the heart of a spirituality for our time is not the blind faith of traditional religion but the rational faith of the modern seeker combined with an abiding sense of the human family, now global in its reach, and of the presence of a higher, creating power. Evolution is often regarded as an atheistic theory, but a poem that the pioneer evolutionist Alfred Russel Wallace quoted in one of his most important essays illustrates that this is untrue. Quite to the contrary, if the perfectly rational hypothesis of a creating power is accepted, however obscure its methods may be in certain ways, one resonates with the hymn to creation that was for Wallace an expression of his deepest sentiments:

> God of the Granite and the Rose!
> Soul of the Sparrow and the Bee!
> The mighty tide of Being flows
> Through countless channels, Lord, from thee.
> It leaps to life in grass and flowers,
> Through every grade of being runs,
> While from Creation's radiant towers
> Its glory flames in Stars and Suns.

The Challenge and the Promise

However distant may be the vision of a higher kind of happiness, this is what an authentic religion for our time must offer a world which is being transformed into a global village by trade, travel and communication. Our inherited prejudices are so deep-rooted, however, that most people will never stop to consider whether a unifying and developmental theology is desirable, let alone possible. It is far easier either to accept unthinkingly either the new atheism or the faith of our fathers.

In the past, tribal consciousness was generated in an unselfconscious way through stories, songs and rituals passed on from generation to generation, learned at the mother's knee and in initiation into adulthood. Later, cultural consciousness was learned much more deliberately through systematic reading of the great religious texts, particularly the Bible by Christians, the "Old Testament" and Mishnah by Jews, the Koran by Moslems, the Gitas, Upanishads and Mabharata by Hindus. Each of these traditions has formed a particular world view, ethical sensitivity, etc., so that we have become, in effect, different human subgroups, each a quasi-species (to borrow Manfred Eigen's term) cut off from the others by our inherited religions and their myths. Most people would accept this mutual alienation as part of the natural order of things, and even those who find it intolerable will probably consider the concept of a global family unrealistic. The only way the situation can be changed is by re-education on a global scale, stepping beyond the scriptures of the past to create a new kind of developmental programme.

A challenge on this scale is daunting, and may well seem to be an impossibility, for there are no institutions to promote it, no universally accepted texts and few enthusiasts. In such a situation one could be easily tempted to dismiss the ideal as impracticable, even assuming that one had accepted it is desirable. Some might fear that it looks forward to a homogenized world, without the cultural variety that gives life such flavour, but there is no reason at all to think that global unity would result in a dull uniformity. Like any normal family, a global family can both contain and enjoy all kinds of diversity. Once the ideal of global unity has been accepted, we shall find that we become increasingly dissatisfied with a situation that previously we had assumed to be unchangeable. Dissatisfaction with the present order is the first step to a higher consciousness.